Faith

ENCOUNTER

Bill Myers & Michael Ross

HARVEST HOUSE PUBLISHERS
Eugene, Oregon 97402

Cover by Terry Dugan Design, Minneapolis, Minnesota

Interior design by Corey Fisher

FAITH ENCOUNTER
Copyright 1999 by Bill Myers and Michael Ross
Published by Harvest House Publishers
Eugene, Oregon 97402

Library of Congress cataloging-in-publication data

Myers, Bill, 1953–
    Faith encounter / Bill Myers and Michael Ross.
        p.   cm.
    ISBN 0-7369-0158-2
    1. Youth Prayer—books and devotions—English.   I. Ross, Michael, 1961–   .
    II. Title.
    BV4850.M96   1999
    248.8'3—dc21   99-21700
                                                                          CIP

00 01 02 03 04 05 06 / BP / 10 9 8 7 6 5 4 3 2

To Greg Johnson

"I have been crucified with Christ
and I no longer live, but Christ lives in me."

Your life models this truth.

Contents

ST ART HERE → Immanuel: God with Us

Immanuel: God with Us

You're about to begin a life-changing journey.

As you read this book and study the four Gospels (Matthew, Mark, Luke, and John), you'll encounter the most amazing man who ever walked the earth—Jesus Christ. You'll also discover the secret to living the ultimate life.

But before we begin, let's clear up a few questions many people have.

For starters, why does the Bible have four different versions of the life of Jesus? Did it take God four different people and four different tries to get it right? And why do the four Gospels often tell the same story, but from four different viewpoints and with different details? Does that mean we really can't believe every word in the Bible?

Unfortunately, many people come to the conclusion that the Bible is unreliable and inconsistent. Yet the Bible says that "all Scripture is God-breathed" (2 Timothy 3:16). It doesn't say some or most, but *all*.

So what gives?

What happens when four honest people tell the same story? You get the truth from four slightly different angles because each person has his or her own way of seeing things and own areas of experience.

The same is true with the Gospels. God makes sure that the details and facts are accurate, but He doesn't turn the writers into robots. He writes the truth through each one of them but allows the men to keep their own personalities, viewpoints, and vocabularies. Matthew is Jewish and uses Old Testament prophecy to prove Jesus is the Messiah, the one Israel has waited so long for. Luke, on the other hand, is a doctor who sees Jesus as the Great Physician who comes to save a sick and diseased world. John, a fisherman, is one of Christ's closest friends. He writes in a simple, easy-to-read style and aims to make the gospel clear to all who read it. He loves to explore the depths of Jesus' teachings. Mark is a let's-cut-to-the-chase, just-the-facts guy. His gospel is a simple, succinct, unadorned—yet vivid—record of Jesus' ministry. Mark emphasizes what Jesus did more than what He said. All four of the gospel accounts— Matthew, Mark, Luke, and John—are totally accurate. By combining them, we get a complete picture of God the Son.

God's Word is the most powerful weapon in the universe—"sharper than any double-edged sword" (Hebrews 4:12). In fact, when Jesus was battling it out with Satan in the wilderness, it was the only weapon He chose to fight with. What makes God's Word—the Bible—so powerful is that it's "God-breathed." Think about that for a minute. God breathed His very life into the words of Scripture. Something with that ultimate authority has to be life-changing. The Bible says that God's Word:

- ✔ cleans us up (Ephesians 5:26)
- ✔ shows us what we're really like (James 1:23-25)
- ✔ encourages us (Romans 15:4)
- ✔ equips us to do good (2 Timothy 3:17)
- ✔ leads us to faith (Romans 10:17)
- ✔ shows us the way to be saved (James 1:21)

Pretty powerful stuff. To get the most out of it, here's what you need to do:

First: Read the Scripture and the portion of Scripture under "Ultimate Word" at the beginning of each section.

Second: Stop a moment and think about what God may be telling you in these verses. Ask God to make it clear to you.

Third: Then go ahead and read the interesting facts and eye-opening insights in this book.

Some people think they'll save time by plowing through the book, just reading the commentary, but they're only fooling themselves. *God's Word does the changing,* not us. Our goal is to help you understand Scripture and get you actively involved in God's Word.

It's a genuine faith encounter with Jesus Christ that will power you up for ultimate living.

Get ready for the ultimate experience!

ULTIMATE Life!

Week One

Journey
to the
scene of
Christ's
birth,
then
fast-
forward
to His
teenage
years and
early
ministry.

Day 1: God Chooses Mary

Then the angel said to her, "Do not be afraid, Mary, for you have found favor with God. And behold, you will conceive in your womb and bring forth a Son, and shall call His name JESUS. He will be great, and will be called the Son of the Highest" (Luke 1:30-32 NKJV).

Ultimate Word: *Read Luke 1:26-38*

Ultimate Encounter

It's safe to believe that Mary is in her early to mid teens since that's the usual marrying age in her culture. So it is to this young woman that Gabriel makes the greatest birth announcement in history: *God is paying an extended visit to mankind.* Mary is told to name her baby Jesus, which means "the Lord is salvation" in Hebrew. Gabriel also promises her Jesus will be God's Son, as well as the Messiah, and His kingdom will last forever!

Mary doesn't doubt or even ask for a sign as proof. Instead, she simply wants to know, "How will this be?" Gabriel explains, and then he gives her a special sign: Elizabeth, her aging relative who couldn't have children is already pregnant!

Mary's response is hard to believe. Being an unwed mother didn't help a woman's popularity too much in those days. And engagements (Mary is engaged to Joseph) were considered much more important than today. They lasted a year and could only be broken with a divorce. Any fooling around on Mary's part would have been considered adultery. So there is the possibility that Joseph will divorce her, and, according to the Mosaic law, she could also face the death penalty (see Deuteronomy 22:23,24).

Mary has good cause to be a bit nervous. But instead of looking at all the possible life-shattering dangers, Mary keeps her eyes fixed on God's faithful love and, in a sense, simply says, "Yes, Lord, I'll trust You."

We can take a clue from Mary. Even when her whole world seemed to turn upside down and her future was fuzzy, she still trusted God. (She knew the "big picture" was crystal clear to God, the Master Artist.)

If you ever visit an art gallery, try this "big picture" experiment. Find a painting you like, then stand really close to it. You'll see nothing but big, confusing blobs of paint. At such a close distance, the artwork will look like one gigantic, horrible mistake. But as you step back from the image you'll suddenly discover how everything fits together and the confusing blobs actually add to the beauty.

Our lives can be the same way. We can be so close to our problems, so involved with them, that we can't see the perfect masterpiece God is creating.

We may not understand why we have to put up with big blobs of confusion in our lives. We may kick and scream a lot. We may even accuse God of making a terrible mistake. But He is the Master Artist. He is the one who stands back and sees the whole picture. He knows exactly what is needed to turn us into beautiful works of art. God doesn't make any mistakes in His creations.

Ultimate Action

Learn to trust the Master Artist just as Mary did. Focus your attention entirely on God—especially during those times when you need help over a seemingly impossible problem. With your eyes fixed firmly on Him, you'll have the strength to make that simple yet courageous statement, "Yes, Lord, I'll trust You."

Day 2: Cosmic Connection

When Elizabeth heard Mary's greeting, the baby leaped in her womb, and Elizabeth was filled with the Holy Spirit. In a loud voice she exclaimed: "Blessed are you among women, and blessed is the child you will bear!" (Luke 1:41, 42).

Ultimate Word: *Read Luke 1:39-80*

Ultimate Encounter

Mary rushes to Elizabeth and Zechariah's place, which is about 65 miles away (not exactly an afternoon stroll). When they meet, Elizabeth's unborn baby leaps for joy as Elizabeth is filled with the Holy Spirit and calls Mary the mother of her Lord. Elizabeth tells Mary how fortunate she is, not because she has done anything on her own, but because she has simply taken God completely at His word and trusted Him.

Mary agrees but makes sure the glory goes to the right person. She praises God for choosing her, for His love that encourages the humble, and for the fact that what's happening isn't a new plan but the fulfillment of an ancient promise.

A few months later, everyone is pretty excited when Elizabeth gives birth to her son, John. But the neighbors can't quite swallow the name. A backyard, over-the-fence conversation may have gone something like this:

What's with this John stuff? Listen, Zech, don't you know the firstborn is named after the father? That's how Jewish people keep the family name going. There's not a single John in your entire family!

But Zechariah isn't about to make the same mistake twice. When the angel Gabriel first told Zechariah that he would be a father, he didn't believe it so his speech was taken from him. The angel also said to name the son John—which is exactly what Zechariah would do! He writes in no uncertain terms, "His name is John." And because of this act of faith, he immediately begins to speak and prophesy about coming events.

What an amazing account of God's faithfulness. Understand that Zechariah could not speak until his actions said, "Yes, I trust You, Lord." Elizabeth called Mary blessed because Mary said, "Yes, I trust You, Lord." In contrast, Adam and Eve blew it (and put the world in the mess it's in) because their actions said, "No, we don't trust You, Lord."

How many times a day do we say, "Yes, I trust You, Lord"? God promises us love, peace, and protection: "And we know that in all things God works for the good of those who love him, who have been called according to his purpose" (Romans 8:28).

But how many times do we fall for Satan's lies? How many times do we feel that if we don't fret, fuss, and worry, whatever we want will not work out for the very best? We need to get a clue: These are Satan's lies!

Ultimate Action

Don't let Satan trip you up. Instead, claim the truth whether you can physically see it at this particular moment or not. As Jesus says, "If you hold to my teaching, you are really my disciples. Then you will know the truth, and the truth will set you free" (John 8:31,32).

Day 3: The King Is Born

There is born to you this day in the city of David a Savior, who is Christ the Lord. And this will be the sign to you: You will find a Babe wrapped in swaddling cloths, lying in a manger (Luke 2:11, 12 NKJV).

Ultimate Word: *Read Luke 2:1-20*

Ultimate Encounter

It doesn't seem like a suitable place for the King of kings: the animals, the filth, the smells, the flies, the dusty, scratchy hay—and having a feeding trough, of all things, for a crib! But God, in His infinite love, chooses the humblest possible surroundings. No one can accuse Jesus of not knowing hardships and pain.

What's more, it's not to the kings, or to the great intellectuals, or even to the celebrities that God sends the ultimate birth announcement. Instead, the Creator of the universe first shares His great joy with simple, humble shepherds. (Apparently high positions don't impress Him too much.) Suddenly, the sky splits apart with "a multitude of the heavenly host praising God" and promising peace on earth to those who please Him (Luke 2:13 NASB).

Meanwhile, Mary remains as obedient as ever, despite the fact that her world has been incredibly shaken. Instead of looking at the stigma of being an unwed mother, she keeps her eyes fixed on God's faithful love and says, "I am the Lord's servant."

Are our eyes fixed on God's faithful love? Can we see beyond our problems to His love? If you're having trouble with that, keep in mind that part of His love involved coming all the way down to our level to live in this dirty, sin-infested world in the person of His Son. Let's move in closer and get a better look at this Son...

No beauty. "He had no beauty or majesty to attract us to him, nothing in his appearance that we should desire him" (Isaiah 53:2).

No reputation. The Bible describes Jesus as one who "made himself nothing, taking the very nature of a servant, being made in human likeness" (Philippians 2:7).

No sin. "God made him who had no sin to be sin for us, so that in him we might become the righteousness of God" (2 Corinthians 5:21).

Ultimate Action

✔ *Focus on Christ's image.* His beauty comes from the inside out. His eyes radiate with unlimited peace; His smile speaks of incomprehensible joy. Most of all, His heart beats with boundless love.

✔ *Accept Christ's friendship.* He won't make fun of your fears or blab your secrets. Instead, He'll be the greatest, most loyal friend you'll ever have.

✔ *Nurture integrity—not popularity.* Even if you become the planet's most popular guy or gal, without Christ it's all pretty empty and pointless. Through your Bible study, praise times, and prayers, let Jesus show you the meaning of *true* acceptance, *true* fulfillment, and *true* hope.

Day 4: Boy Savior

After three days they found him in the temple courts, sitting among the teachers, listening to them and asking them questions. Everyone who heard him was amazed at his understanding and his answers (Luke 2:46,47).

Ultimate Word: *Read Luke 2:39-52*

Ultimate Encounter

At age 12, a Jewish boy becomes more responsible for his actions. No longer can he get by with saying, "Hey, I'm just a kid" or "I didn't know any better." Jesus is 12, nearly 13, when He goes to the Feast of the Passover in Jerusalem with His parents.

Jerusalem is about 65 miles from Nazareth, so after the seven-day festival, Mary and Joseph join a caravan (it's usually safer to travel in a large group) and head home. As a rule, the women leave earlier in the morning because they walk slower and have children to contend with. Then the men leave, and the two groups meet and camp together in the evening.

During the journey, Mary probably figures Jesus is with Joseph, while Joseph figures He's with her. It's quite a shock when they get together in the evening and discover He isn't with either of them! Mary and Joseph comb the camp looking for Him, then spend three days searching the streets of Jerusalem. They hit all the festival attractions that should interest a boy of Jesus' age. The last place they'd expect to find Him is in the temple. But there He is, politely listening and asking questions of the top teachers and amazing all of them with His solid insights and answers.

Mary is naturally upset and asks Jesus why He's being so inconsiderate.

Jesus' response? "Why were you searching for me?... Didn't you know I had to be in my Father's house?"

These are the earliest words of Jesus quoted in the New Testament. Before this time, no one had ever used the term "My Father" as Jesus had. No one had ever referred to the Creator in such a personal, intimate way. If we reread Jesus' words, we discover two things about our young Messiah:

1. *He knows who He is.* No cruising into the turbulent teen years with an identity crisis. No giving into peer pressure or experimenting with the dark side of life. Jesus accepts who He is and stays true to His identity.

2. *He knows His life's mission.* Best of all, He accepts it. Keep in mind that Jesus is fully God *and* fully human. Yet He keeps His frail, human side in check and stays committed to His calling.

One more amazing thing happens: Jesus returns home with His parents and remains obedient to them. The fact that He's God's Son doesn't give Him the right to rebel.

Ultimate Action

✔ *Don't lose your identity.* In the world's eyes, your identity is wrapped up in what you do, how smart or athletic you are, and how you look. But in God's eyes, what matters is who you are—His child.

✔ *Find your identity in Christ.* Our Lord wants the very best for you. His plans for you are even better than your wildest dreams. Jesus doesn't look at you and say, "This is who you are, and who you'll always be." Instead, He says, "Just imagine who you can become!"

Day 5: Repent or Perish!

"I baptize with water," John replied, "but among you stands one you do not know. He is the one who comes after me, the thongs of whose sandals I am not worthy to untie" (John 1:26,27).

Ultimate Word: *Read John 1:19-28*

Ultimate Encounter

John the Baptist is drawing such a crowd that the religious hotshots figure they'd better pay a little visit to check him out. Keep in mind that everyone is waiting for the Messiah to appear. The Savior of Israel has been promised by God for thousands of years, so the crowd is expecting Him to make His debut any minute. It's little wonder, then, that the first question out of the authorities' mouths is, "Are you the Christ?"

John's answer couldn't be clearer: "No way!"

Next they ask if he is Elijah, the Old Testament prophet who was whisked up to heaven hundreds of years ago (a guy many thought would come back to announce the Christ).

Again John says no.

Next, they ask if he's the prophet (somebody a lot of folks also thought would be showing up).

Wrong again.

In desperation, they throw out the true-or-false quiz and get right to the point: "Who are you?"

He answers by quoting from Isaiah, an Old Testament prophet who spent a lot of time writing about the coming

Messiah: "I am the voice of one calling in the desert, 'Make straight the way for the Lord' " (John 1:23). In other words, "It's my job to tell you to straighten out your lives because God's on His way!"

At this point, the bigwigs are getting a little hot under the collar. They came to grill John, not to be preached at. So they demand to know, "If you're just a nobody, then who do you think you are baptizing all these people? Who gave you the authority?"

John gives them an answer, but not the one they're expecting. He says that standing right there among them is somebody they don't know—somebody whose sandals he's not even fit to untie.

For what it's worth, John's not talking about being a shoe salesperson here. Untying sandals was considered such a low-level job that only slaves were supposed to do it. So John makes it pretty clear that he's not out there on some ego trip. Instead, he's there to prepare the people for somebody else—somebody he's not even fit to be a slave to.

Needless to say, he's got everyone's attention.

It had to be a pretty strange sight. John the Baptist was out roasting in the desert, wearing camel-hair clothing, eating locusts and wild honey, and telling people they'd better get their acts together because God was on His way.

Yet there was something about John the Baptist that people were taking seriously. He struck a universal chord—one that still rings true today. He hit upon an intangible feeling of guilt, a deep-rooted sense that somehow humanity has failed. More importantly, the people of the world needed to find a way to wash themselves from these failures—to be cleansed from these sins.

John the Baptist was pointing to the answer: *Jesus Christ*.

Ultimate Action

✔ *Give up the performance trap.* Following the letter of the law and trying to be a good person won't bring you life. Only God's love and mercy can do that.

✔ *Stop reliving old sins.* And stop thinking that you just can't cut it as a Christian. If you've confessed your sins to Jesus and have committed your life to Him, you are forgiven and free! Not only free from punishment, but if you let Him, He can actually free you from sinning! That's definitely *ultimate* life!

Day 6: Spirit-Filled Son

When He had been baptized, Jesus came up immediately from the water; and behold, the heavens were opened to Him, and He saw the Spirit of God descending like a dove and alighting upon Him. And suddenly a voice came from heaven, saying, "This is My beloved Son, in whom I am well pleased" (Matthew 3:16,17 NKJV).

Ultimate Word: *Read Matthew 3:13-17*

Ultimate Encounter

John the Baptist can't believe what he's hearing. His cousin Jesus just asked to be baptized by him. Imagine that!

"I need to be baptized by you, and do you come to me?" John asks.

Jesus isn't kidding, He means what He says: "Let it be so now; it is proper for us to do this to fulfill all righteousness." Jesus knows He doesn't need to be cleansed, but He points out that He needs to identify fully with the people to whom He was sent. What's more, His Father has chosen this occasion to publicly declare that Jesus is the Son of God: "This is my Son, whom I love," God's voice booms from heaven, "with him I am well pleased."

It's a moment that will live forever. Heaven opens, the Father speaks, and the Spirit of God descends on Jesus like a dove. It's the first time since Creation that God publicly reveals His amazing nature: Three persons in one—the

Father (the voice), the Son (Jesus), and the Holy Spirit (in the form of a dove); all three forms, yet only one God.

Astonishing!

Now for the obvious question: "How can one God be in three forms?" This is a biggie. It's a question that's given mankind headaches for centuries (probably because of our limited capacity to comprehend). One good way to understand God is by looking at a man.

A man can be a *son* to his parents, a *father* to his children, and a *husband* to his wife. He's all three things at once, but he's still one person. We have one God, but He's three persons.

Another way of tackling this question is by taking a look at water (H_2O). Even though it can be found in three separate forms—ice, liquid, steam—it will always remain H_2O. The same is true of God. He can take on three forms, but He will always remain one God.

Ultimate Action

✔ *Be in awe of God.* Spend some time praying to Him, thanking Him for His awesome nature and for coming to earth to save humanity. Ask Him to help you trust Him more each day.

✔ *Take comfort in God's presence.* Know that He is with you at all times. Ask Him to help you seek His voice and to depend on His guidance.

Day 7: The Master's Plan

The next day John saw Jesus coming toward him and said, "Look, the Lamb of God, who takes away the sin of the world! This is the one I meant when I said, 'A man who comes after me has surpassed me because he was before me'" (John 1:29,30).

Ultimate Word: *Read John 1:29-34*

Ultimate Encounter

"Look, the Lamb of God!"

At first, John the Baptist's description of the Lord seems a bit strange to the ear. After all, he could have said, "Look, the Creator of the universe! It's God—the one and only. Drop to your knees, folks; it's supreme ruler time!" But John, under the inspiration of the Holy Spirit, uses an interesting word picture—a lamb—when he introduces Jesus. John the Baptist knows the Master's plan, and he doesn't want anyone to miss it.

If John insists upon comparing Jesus to an animal, why not: "Behold, the Roaring Lion" or "Behold, the Soaring Eagle"? Why some ninth-rated animal like a baby sheep?

First of all, it was lambs that were used in the temple sacrifice. Every day a lamb was killed in the morning, then another in the evening to pay for people's sins. This sounds pretty cruel, but keep in mind that sin is pretty cruel. In fact, it's deadly—and somebody has to pay for it. And, as unfair as it seems, it's better that an animal pay with its life than a human.

So, in one sense, John is saying, "Look, this is the Lamb God has supplied. This is the one who will suffer and die in our place for all our sins."

Another reason the analogy works is that the blood from lambs is what saved the people of Israel just before the exodus, when they were getting ready to leave Egypt. Remember? Despite all the miracles God was performing through Moses, Pharaoh would not let the Israelites leave. So finally, to get His point across, God made plans to wipe out all of the firstborn in the country. There was one problem: The Israelites had a few firstborn, too. How could they be protected while God carried out His judgment on the Egyptians?

The solution was simple. To be saved, the Israelites were to kill lambs and smear their blood over their doors. Later that night, when the Angel of Death went from house to house to kill the firstborn, he'd see the blood over the Israelites' doorways and literally *pass over* the homes that were covered by the blood.

It's Jesus' blood that saves us from eternal death.

Ultimate Action

Pause for a moment and consider John the Baptist's message. In essence he is saying, "Look, here's someone who will take all of your sins—every failure, everything you've ever done wrong—and dispose of them forever. He will take all that guilt, all that blame upon Himself. He will take the punishment that should be yours so you can be clean, so you can be free."

Do you believe the Master's plan? Jesus came to take away your sins so you can live forever. He is the *only answer* to your sin dilemma. He is the one through whom you can experience grace. Eternal life is yours for the asking....But you *have* to ask.

ULTIMATE Relationship!

Encounter
Christ's plan
to destroy
meaningless
religion and
replace it
with a
life-giving
relationship—
a relationship
with God.

Day 8: Desert Training

Then Jesus was led up by the Spirit into the wilderness to be tempted by the devil. And when He had fasted forty days and forty nights, afterward He was hungry. Now when the tempter came to Him, he said, "If You are the Son of God, command that these stones become bread" (Matthew 4:1-3 NKJV).

Ultimate Word: *Read Matthew 4:1-11*

Ultimate Encounter

Talk about stress! If Jesus slips up just once, commits even one little sin, it's all over. God will no longer have the perfect sacrifice to live and die in our place—and the world cannot be saved. Satan knows this. So he uses all of his strength and cunning to get Jesus to stumble just once.

Jesus has spent 40 days and nights in the wilderness with no food. That's nearly six weeks! Naturally, He is hungry. And Satan is there with his first phase of attack: the temptation of immediate self-gratification.

"If You are the Son of God, command that these stones become bread," he says to Jesus.

The trick fails, so Satan goes into phase two of testing God. He takes Jesus to the highest point of the temple and challenges Him to jump since it is written that "[God] will command his angels concerning you, and they will lift you up in their hands…" (Matthew 4:6).

Jesus makes it clear that there's one person you *never* test—God.

Finally, Satan goes to plan three. "All this I will give you, if you will bow down and worship me." (He encourages us to compromise and we'll have it made. One lie, and our parents will be off our cases. Cheat a little, and we'll get good grades.)

But Satan fails again as Jesus resists. "Away with you, Satan!" Jesus says. "For it is written: 'You shall worship the Lord your God, and Him only you shall serve' " (NKJV).

Satan attacked Jesus hard and heavy. And for good reason—He was fighting for the very world. But each time, a physically exhausted Jesus won. How? He had powerful ammunition—a weapon that's available to us today—the Word of God. Satan tells us to satisfy our physical desires; let those desires take control. Why wait for marriage to have sex? Why turn down those drugs? Why refuse an extra piece of cake? If it feels good, do it! But God says to resist the devil—just like Jesus did, with God's Word, and he will flee.

Ultimate Action

Jesus didn't launch a nuclear missile at Satan. He didn't fight with guns or tanks. Instead He relied on Scripture. There's a definite supernatural power in the Word of God. The book of Ephesians lists the armor we're to wear when we go into battle against the enemy. Most of the items are defensive. The only offensive weapon we need is "the sword of the Spirit, which is the word of God" (Ephesians 6:17).

Day 9: John Follows Jesus

As Jesus was walking beside the Sea of Galilee, he saw two brothers, Simon called Peter and his brother Andrew. They were casting a net into the lake, for they were fishermen. "Come, follow me," Jesus said, "and I will make you fishers of men." At once they left their nets and followed him (Matthew 4:18-20).

Ultimate Word: *Read Matthew 4:18-22*

Ultimate Encounter

Fishing is your life. You're barely an adult, yet you're convinced that throwing nets into the sea and landing the big catch is the way to make a living. Not only does it put food on the table, but it's sort of the family thing to do.

Little do you realize that God has a bigger catch in mind.

One day, while preparing nets as usual with your dad and brother, something amazing happens—an encounter that changes your life forever!

Just off in the distance, not too far away, you spot a man walking along the shore. He's definitely no ordinary guy. There's something about His face—a gentleness, a strength, an unconditional love that you've never before experienced. And His voice—it's amazing. "Follow me!" That's all He says. "Follow me!"

Something deep inside compels you to do the extraordinary: You immediately leave behind the security of your old life and find something—*someone!*—even greater.

You encounter the Messiah!

How do we know Jesus is really the Messiah? How do we know He's really the Son of God?

If anyone knew Jesus, the disciple John did. Not only was he a member of the "Big Twelve," but he was also one of Jesus' closest friends. In fact, he was one of only three people with Jesus when God the Father dropped by for a little social call (see Luke 9:28-36). John was the only one Jesus asked to look after His mother when He was dying on the cross. And he was the only person Jesus appeared to when He described the end times in the book of Revelation.

Talk about connected. And this apostle wastes no time in the book of John. He gets right to the point and begins by calling Jesus God: "In the beginning was the Word, and the Word was with God, and the Word was God" (John 1:1).

Talk about gutsy. John's either trying to pull off one of the biggest con jobs in history—or he's stating an amazing fact. And if it's the latter, then there had better be plenty of other Scriptures to back it up. Fortunately for John (and us) there are. The apostle Paul wrote:

✔ "Your attitude should be the same as that of Christ Jesus: Who, being in very nature God, did not consider equality with God something to be grasped, but made himself nothing, taking the very nature of a servant, being made in human likeness" (Philippians 2:5-7).

✔ "For by him all things were created: things in heaven and on earth, visible and invisible, whether thrones or powers or rulers or authorities; all things were created by him and for him" (Colossians 1:16).

✔ "For in Christ all the fullness of the Deity lives in bodily form, and you have been given fullness in Christ, who is the head over every power and authority" (Colossians 2:9).

Because of John's close relationship with Jesus, it's no big surprise that John's account of Jesus' life is one of the most popular books in the Bible. As we read John's writings, we can't help but notice that John really loved Jesus. His solid faith helped to turn the world upside down. John had a faith that he wasn't afraid to boast about.

Ultimate Action

Like John, don't be afraid to leave behind the so-called security of your old life and embrace the radical new life Jesus has for you. What's more, don't be ashamed of the good news of the gospel. The Lord gave John—and you—an important mission: Tell the world about Jesus Christ, our Savior, and the gift of eternal life He offers to everyone. John placed this awesome assignment above everything, including ridicule, peer pressure, popularity, and even the possibility of losing friends. Do you?

Day 10: Faithful Few

Jesus answered and said to him, "Because I said to you that I saw you under the fig tree, do you believe? You shall see greater things than these....You shall see the heavens opened, and the angels of God ascending and descending on the Son of Man" (John 1:50,51 NASB).

Ultimate Word: *Read John 1:35-51*

Ultimate Encounter

Soon people begin to follow Jesus. In fact, Jesus' first two disciples were originally John the Baptist's disciples. Then Peter, Philip, and Nathanael sign up. Note that not one of these men is convinced to follow Jesus by any great philosophical debate or argument. Instead, it is the simple declaration of who Jesus is (by John the Baptist) or the gentle encouragement (once by Jesus and once by Philip) to "come and see."

You can't argue anybody into accepting Jesus as Savior. No amount of mental gymnastics or verbal overkill will do the trick. It has to be something God shows them; it has to be something they decide on their own.

If you're reading this and don't know if you're ready for all this "Jesus stuff," don't expect what you read in this

book to convince you. Don't expect your friends or relatives to convince you. That's between you and God. They
can help you understand the gospel, but you need to check
God out for yourself. "Come and see"; ask *Him* to show
you if He's real. And if you're serious, He will. It may not
be overnight, but if you start reading His Word and asking
Him to reveal Himself, He will.

On the other hand, if you're already a believer and want
to see your friends and relatives saved, don't cram it down
their throats. Look for opportunities to share your faith,
yes, but don't try to con or fast-talk them into the kingdom.
You're not selling used cars here; you're offering people
friendship with God. And friendship is not something you
can argue anyone into. A man does not argue a woman into
loving him. Likewise, a woman does not argue a man into
marrying her. A couple's love and commitment to each
other comes as a result of knowing and trusting each other.
It's also that way with a person's relationship with God.

When Nathanael tried to pull Philip into a debate, when
he hit him with, "Nazareth! Can anything good come from
there?" Philip's only response was, "Come and see."

Ultimate Action

When you talk to friends and loved ones, encourage
them to get to know God and to read His Word. Ask
them to look at what He's done in their lives. Explain
what "the Lamb of God" did for us on the cross. *And
pray for them!* But don't turn your witnessing into a
big philosophical argument. Debates and fast-talking
are for politicians and con artists—not for loving
people and sharing Christ with them.

Day 11: Water to Wine

Jesus said to the servants, "Fill the jars with water"; so they filled them to the brim. Then he told them, "Now draw some out and take it to the master of the banquet." They did so, and the master of the banquet tasted the water that had been turned into wine. He did not realize where it had come from, though the servants who had drawn the water knew (John 2:7-9).

Ultimate Word: *Read John 2:1-11*

Ultimate Encounter

Now before anyone uses this water-to-wine miracle as an excuse to grab a six-pack and put down a few cold ones, let's get the whole picture. For starters, Scripture makes it pretty clear that drinking and believing don't mix: "Do not get drunk" (Ephesians 5:18).

Again and again, the Bible talks about the dangers and stupidity of getting drunk. If you have any doubts, take a look at how God ranks drunkenness: "The acts of the sinful nature are obvious: sexual immorality, impurity and debauchery; idolatry and witchcraft; hatred, discord, jealousy, fits of rage, selfish ambition, dissensions, factions and envy; *drunkenness*, orgies, and the like. I warn you, as I did before, that *those who live like this will not inherit the kingdom of God*" (Galatians 5:19-21, emphasis added).

But if God's down on getting drunk, why, of all things, did He choose to turn water into wine for His very first miracle? And we're not talking a few glasses here. We're talking 180 gallons worth!

First of all, Jesus' showing up at the celebration makes it pretty clear that He's not a pious killjoy: "Excuse me, are you having fun? Well, I'm sorry—you'll have to find another religion."

But it doesn't make Him a party animal either.

What it *does* show is that He is perfectly comfortable celebrating and rejoicing with others at a wedding feast. The idea that He is a scowling, Bible-thumping, down-with-good-times fanatic just doesn't fit into the picture Scripture paints.

Second, running out of food or refreshments at a celebration of this importance would be pretty embarrassing. For months the newlyweds would be the joke of the town. Not exactly the way to start off a new life together. So Jesus, in His sympathy and understanding, chooses to take care of the little problem. (It's nice to know that even the little embarrassments of our lives are important to Him.)

But there's a third reason. The water in those stone pots was used to wash the people's hands and feet as part of a Jewish religious ceremony, a routine that was anything but interesting. So by changing that water into wine, Jesus was making another clear statement. In essence He was saying, "I'm taking this dead, boring religion of yours and transforming it into something that is sparkling, something that is exciting and full of life!" That's what Christ came to do. He came to do away with "religion." That's right. He came to destroy meaningless ritual and replace it with a dynamic, on-fire relationship—a relationship with God Himself.

Jesus said, "I have come that they may have life, and have it *to the full*" (John 10:10, emphasis added).

Ultimate Action

The choice is yours: Keep Christianity as just a religion—boring and dull, playing it safe, going through the ceremonial motions and traditions of "churchianity"—or begin pursuing Jesus and drinking His new wine. Begin taking Him up on His promises. Begin stepping out and putting His Word to the test in *all* areas of your life. In short, you can begin living on that water-walking, cutting edge of His power. And once that's happened, once you've tasted that new wine, your life will never be the same!

Day 12: Housecleaning Time

Now the Passover of the Jews was at hand, and Jesus went up to Jerusalem. And He found in the temple those who sold oxen and sheep and doves, and the money changers doing business. When He had made a whip of cords, He drove them all out of the temple, with the sheep and the oxen, and poured out the changers' money and overturned the tables (John 2:13-15 NKJV).

Ultimate Word: *Read John 2:12-25*

Ultimate Encounter

Today's Scripture is serious business. We can learn a lot about Jesus in His zeal to drive the money changers out of the temple. Let's break it down into three major points.

Salvation Is Serious

John shatters the idea that God is some kindly old duffer who shuffles around heaven passing out hugs and kisses. True, God *is* love. But for those who want to rebel—or worse yet, those who rip off His kids—well, let's just say He's got another plan.

That's what we see in this passage. People would travel hundreds of miles to Jerusalem to worship God, only to discover their money was not good enough to give to the temple—or their animals were not good enough to sacrifice.

But, hey, no sweat. Luckily for them, there just happens to be dozens of people inside the temple court who will gladly exchange their "dirty" money for "clean" money or sell them "acceptable" animals for sacrifice. But one of the major problems is that these merchants make up to 1,800-percent profit in the process!

No wonder Jesus is steamed. (And His feelings haven't changed.) For those who want to follow Him and who want to help their fellow human beings—there's love and understanding. For those who exploit and step all over people—there's still the whip.

Christ Is King

After the housecleaning, people begin grilling Jesus about who He thinks He is. Pulling off the stunt He did calls for some pretty high authority. If He's claiming to be the Christ, He'd better get to it and make His point by impressing everyone with a few miracles.

But God won't be bullied. He'll never be manipulated. His miracles are for loving, healing, and encouraging. They are never to entertain or wow the curious. So instead of putting on a sideshow, Jesus prophesies about His upcoming resurrection. But, as is usually the case with spiritual truth, the people miss the boat. They think He's talking about an immediate, literal interpretation: "You're going to rebuild our temple in *how* many days?" They aren't expecting His deeper, change-all-the-rules, eternal truth: "In three days I'll raise this temple, My body, from the dead to prove I'm telling the truth about Myself. I'll be doing this to demonstrate a purer, more powerful form of worship—a worship where God will no longer be living inside a temple, but will actually be living inside of people.

The Messiah on a Mission

We read that Jesus finally begins to do a few miracles and, as a result, some of the people start to believe He's the Christ. But He knows what they're really thinking. He knows that if He lets them have their way, they'll try to set Him up as a political king. He knows that they don't understand the deeper type of rulership He has in mind—the rulership over people's hearts.

How many times have you heard people hawk Christianity as if it were "Dr. Johnson's Magic Cure-All"?

> Yes siree-bob, just say the magic words, "I believe," and I guarantee you more riches than you'll ever be able to spend, more joy than your circuits can handle, and so much peace and happiness—why, you'll think you've already died and gone to glory!

Then, when disaster strikes, the people feel ripped off, as if God's somehow cheated them. But Jesus never promised us carefree lives without storms. And He certainly never said we'd giggle our way into heaven. He promised us wealth—but a spiritual wealth; a wealth that overflows from inside. He promised us peace—but an inner peace that remains no matter how ugly the outward circumstances may get. And He promised us joy—but a joy that comes from experiencing God's love.

These are the areas that Christ wants to bless and be king over.

Ultimate Action

Let the King be king. Sure, He's in charge of all the outward circumstances in your life. But first and foremost, He's interested in ruling your heart. Once your heart has been changed and filled, pleasing God and doing His will gets a lot easier!

Day 13: Relationship, Not Rules

One Sabbath Jesus was going through the grain-fields, and his disciples began to pick some heads of grain, rub them in their hands and eat the kernels. Some of the Pharisees asked, "Why are you doing what is unlawful on the Sabbath?" (Luke 6:1,2).

Ultimate Word: *Read Luke 6:1-11*

Ultimate Encounter

"Why are you doing what is unlawful on the Sabbath?" It's a question the Messiah is going to hear a lot during His ministry. You see, the Pharisees are stuck on rules, and they just don't understand that Christ is into relationships. In fact, Jesus is here to replace the world's rotting old rules with love—His perfect, life-giving, eternal love.

Jesus' answer should stop the Pharisees in their tracks: "The Son of Man is Lord of the Sabbath." Yet these stubborn religious leaders think they know what's right. After all, the Pharisees invented thousands of additions to God's laws to try to make themselves appear more holy. The trouble is, they've been doing it for so long that they've forgotten what it is like to let God run the show. Again and again we see Jesus reminding them that God is love, not lists and lists of rules.

God doesn't force anyone to accept His gift of eternal life. That decision is always ours. He never sends anyone to hell; we alone make that decision. After hearing the gospel, we choose our final destination. And, as painful as it may be to Him, God always honors our decision, our freedom of choice.

Still, in that incredible love of His, He continually offers the gift. He waits for us with a big smile on His face and His arms open wide. That's some love!

Ultimate Action

It's pretty obvious that Christians aren't perfect—just forgiven. After all, Christ came to save the sick, not the righteous. But too many Christians put rules before relationship. This is called legalism. The next time you get turned off by a legalistic Christian, take your frustration to the Father. Ask Jesus to help you steer clear of bitterness and stay on the right track—the one that leads to an abundant, growing relationship with Him.

Day 14: Christ Shows Compassion

And a leper came to Him, beseeching Him and falling on his knees before Him, and saying to Him, "If You are willing, You can make me clean." And moved with compassion, He stretched out His hand, and touched him, and said to him, "I am willing; be cleansed." And immediately the leprosy left him and he was cleansed (Mark 1:40-42 NASB).

Ultimate Word: *Read Mark 1:40-45*

Ultimate Encounter

The outcast knows he doesn't have a minute to waste. This is his only hope. He must reach the center of town. Not making it there means destruction, the eternal end to an already pitiful life. So the man covers his hideous physique in a smelly wrap and steps out of a dark alley. Suddenly a scream, followed by those inevitable, piercing words: "Stay away, you unclean man...you *leper.*"

Everywhere he goes, the man faces rejection. But that doesn't stop him. He ignores the painful words and continues to hobble along the hot, dusty road—eventually reaching a crowd at the end of the road. Standing among the people is the only person who won't reject him; a man who has the power to make him well. Right there—speaking to the lost, the lonely, the desperate—is a man named Jesus.

And when the leper reaches Jesus, a most incredible thing happens. The leper falls on his knees and begs, "If you are willing, you can make me clean."

Filled with compassion, Jesus reaches out his hand and touches the man. "I am willing," Jesus says. "Be clean!" And immediately the leprosy leaves the man, and the man is cured.

The leper wasn't just some no-name person who got a second chance at life. This outcast represents you and me. His repulsive, deadly disease symbolizes a sickness that plagues us all. Every human who ever lived—except Christ, of course—has a condition that's even worse than leprosy. It's deadly and can kill both the body and the soul. It's a condition called sin.

But there is one cure—Jesus Christ.

When the Great Physician reached out His hand and said, "I am willing," He was also talking to you and me. Even though we are all flawed by a sinful nature, we can be forgiven by Jesus Christ. If we seek out the Savior and ask to be healed, He is willing and able and faithful.

He will lead us along a new road—an eternal journey that's filled with hope, contentment, and purpose.

So what's holding us back?

Ultimate Action

✔ *Know that you are forgiven.* Our Lord stretches out His hand and says, "I am willing...are you?"

✔ *Know where you are headed.* Where is your life right now? Do you feel like an empty shell that's just wasting away? Are you facing major rejection everywhere you turn? Take Christ's hand. He's offering you a whole new life with Him.

ULTIMATE Truth!

Week Three

X

Jesus is
"living
water" and
offers all
who follow Him
real peace,
real
satisfaction,
real
wholeness—
real life.

Day 15: Miracle Messiah

And again He entered Capernaum after some days, and it was heard that He was, in the house....Then they came to Him, bringing a paralytic who was carried by four men. And when they could not come near Him because of the crowd, they uncovered the roof where He was. So when they had broken through, they let down the bed on which the paralytic was lying (Mark 2:1,3-5 NKJV).

Ultimate Word: *Read Mark 2:1-12*

Ultimate Encounter

"Hey, guys! He's here! Right here in our town performing miracles. Let's go check Him out."

News travels fast about the "Miracle Messiah," who is healing the sick and stirring up the crowds with His radical ideas. Even a few of the skeptical religious leaders (the Pharisees) want to hear for themselves. So they make their way into a crowded building and listen with disgust.

Who is this guy? they ask themselves.

The young Jew before them claims to be the Savior. He even insists that He has all authority on earth, yet He wanders the land like a drifter. What's more, He's a mere carpenter's son and hangs out with society's undesirables: lepers, beggars, prostitutes, and traitors.

Suddenly...*Creak! Snap! Crash!* Wood breaks, clay falls, dust rises.

The Pharisees glare.

Jesus smiles.

A paralytic is lowered from the roof and gently placed at Christ's feet.

"Son," Jesus says, "your sins are forgiven."

"Why does this fellow talk like that?" question the teachers of the law. *"He's blaspheming! Who can forgive sins but God alone?"*

Jesus looks at the Pharisees. "Why are you thinking these things," He asks. "But that you may know that the Son of Man has authority on earth to forgive sins..."

Jesus turns to the crippled man. "I tell you, get up, take your mat and go home."

A miracle! The crowd gasps as the paralytic stands up and walks out the door. Everyone in the room rejoices. The teachers of the law are stunned.

Is this man truly who he claims to be?

Jesus became nothing so we could have everything. He wore a crown of thorns so that we might wear a crown of glory. He ate with people so we could someday dine with God. He became sin so that we might become righteousness. He cried tears on earth so we would never shed them in heaven. He walked over dusty roads so we could walk on golden streets.

He died so that we might live.

It's time to let Jesus heal your paralyzed legs and feet so you can leap for joy—and into action, telling the world about this amazing, miracle Messiah.

Ultimate Action

Commit to living fully for Christ. He knows everything about you—even your sinful nature. Yet He still loves you and wants you to experience His love, forgiveness, and power in *all* areas of your life. Experiencing His love does not mean that all of your thoughts, emotions, and behaviors will immediately be pure. What it does mean is that you can be *real*, feeling pain and joy, love and anger, confidence and confusion, knowing Jesus will never reject you. He will always be helping you to overcome any evil. Why? So that your life will be abundant, so you will be whole and complete, not lacking in anything.

Now that's life!

Day 16: Matthew Meets His Maker

Once again Jesus went out beside the lake. A large crowd came to him, and he began to teach them. As he walked along, he saw Levi son of Alphaeus sitting at the tax collector's booth. "Follow me," Jesus told him, and Levi got up and followed him (Mark 2:13,14).

Ultimate Word: *Read Mark 2:13-17*

Ultimate Encounter

His day begins as any other—routine, predictable, most definitely lonely. You see, Matthew is one Jewish man who isn't too popular with his peers. In fact, most people detest him. Matthew has the thankless job of collecting taxes for the Roman government, which spells trouble for everyone (except the Romans) living in first-century Palestine. (The Jewish people live under bondage to Roman taxes, and many tax collectors are less than honest. The people consider guys like Matthew to be traitors and vile sinners.)

As he takes a seat at the tax collector's booth, Matthew has no idea that his life is about to be transformed forever! A man walking by yells out an offer. It has nothing to do with paying taxes.

"Follow me." That's all the man says. "Follow me."

Matthew can't resist. He knows that he has just met an extraordinary man, a man he'll come to know as Messiah.

The decision to follow Christ plunges Matthew into the greatest adventure of all: life as a Christian. Matthew goes on to be the author of an in-depth account of Jesus' life and ministry—the longest of the four Gospels, and one that's packed with details.

One thing is certain about Matthew's life: He's convinced that he encountered the Messiah, and he wants the world to know this Man who says, "I have not come to call the righteous, but sinners" (Mark 2:17).

Ultimate Action

✔ *Disconnect from the world's lies.* "There is a way that seems right to a man, but in the end it leads to death" (Proverbs 16:25).

✔ *Plug into the truth.* Don't be afraid to trust Jesus with your whole heart. Ask Him to help you steer clear of the world's lies and to be firmly grounded in His truth.

✔ *Set off on the ultimate adventure—follow Christ!* Being a committed Christian is the most fulfilling lifestyle anybody could ever hope to experience. Even when problems hit, your heavenly Father is right there with you, helping you overcome life's hardships. *Trust Him!*

Day 17: Born Again

Jesus answered, "Truly, truly, I say to you, unless one is born of water and the Spirit, he cannot enter into the kingdom of God" (John 3:5 NASB).

Ultimate Word: *Read John 3:1-8*

Ultimate Encounter

Now that you've read about Nicodemus, don't come down too hard on him. Keep in mind that throughout his entire life, he has basically interpreted the world in physical terms. Even though he's a religious leader and should have some understanding of what God does in the supernatural, he's thinking and living only in the natural world. No wonder he's a little nervous when he's told he has to be "born again." He's obviously not really happy about having to reexperience the birth process or breaking the news to his mom.

We live and think so much in the natural world that we find God's supernatural interventions a little confusing. We wind up looking at Christianity as a religious code full of do's and don'ts, instead of seeing it as a supernatural relationship with God.

For most of us, trying to understand this relationship and empowering is like being blind and trying to understand the concept of color. If you've never had sight, how can you understand the color blue? "Just tell me what blue sounds like. No? Well then, how about its taste? All right, all right—then just tell me what blue feels like." Obviously none of these descriptions work too well. Sight is different from our other senses, just as touch is different from taste, hearing different from smell, and the spiritual different from the physical.

Jesus tries to make salvation as simple to understand as possible. He explains that to enter the kingdom of God, to experience all of the Lord's gifts both now (while we're alive on earth) and later (in heaven), we have to be "born again." Not a bad description. Just as we had to be born in the flesh to enter our flesh-and-bone lives, we have to be born in the spirit to enter our spiritual lives. But this does not happen by itself.

Contrary to what New Age and Eastern mystics teach, we are *not* born as "one with God and the universe." In actuality, we are born *cut off* from God. We are born spiritually unplugged from our power source.

Why? It's that ugly thing called sin.

But the moment that sin is paid for—the moment we ask Jesus to be our Savior and to come inside our lives to rule—right then, our spiritual lives are born. Those previously dead parts of our lives, our spirits, are suddenly energized. They suddenly come to life. We have joined God's family and are part of His kingdom!

Ultimate Action

Give yourself time to grow. Committing your life to Christ doesn't mean instant maturity. When a baby is born, he or she doesn't immediately understand and function as a full-scale human. It takes time. But gradually, as you feed your spirit and grow, the spiritual things begin to make more and more sense.

Day 18: The Final Decision

For God so loved the world, that He gave His only begotten Son, that whoever believes in Him should not perish, but have eternal life. For God did not send the Son into the world to judge the world, but that the world should be saved through Him.

He who believes in Him is not judged; he who does not believe has been judged already, because he has not believed in the name of the only begotten Son of God (John 3:16-18 NASB).

Ultimate Word: *Read John 3:9-21*

Ultimate Encounter

Nicodemus' story continues. He's still having a hard time understanding this "born again" business, so Jesus tries another approach. Since Nicodemus is a Pharisee and knows the Old Testament backward and forward, Jesus uses an example from it to try to help Nicodemus understand what He's talking about.

Back in Old Testament times, when the people rebelled against God, the Lord sent a plague of poisonous snakes as punishment. The only way they could be saved from this punishment was by looking at a bronze snake Moses had made and put high up on a pole for everyone to see. It was a simple request. All they had to do to be saved was to look at the bronze snake. Once they did, they were healed. What could be easier? (See Numbers 21:4-9.)

To be saved, all people have to do is look at Jesus. That was the whole reason He came—to save us—so, of course, He would make it as simple as possible. And yet people still refuse. Why? Especially when there's a clearcut way of getting right with God and becoming His friend? Why would anyone want to ignore Him?

It could be a matter of ignorance, but that excuse can't last forever. God makes it crystal clear to most people who hear the gospel that they need to receive Jesus as their Savior. But, according to Christ, if they continue to refuse His offer, it's really because they just don't want that friendship with God. They like sin too much. In fact, some people actually prefer living in the darkness of sin to living in the light of God. And, being the gracious God He is, once people have made that final decision, He will honor it—forever.

Ultimate Action

Sometime this week, read Romans 5 and 8. As you study these Scriptures, understand that the Christian's faith is grounded in love: God's love for you and your love for Him. And the best news of all? No one and no thing can separate you from God's love. Here are some questions to think about:

✔ What has Christ come into the world to abolish?

✔ What gives you the confidence that nothing will ever destroy God's love for you?

✔ What does it mean to be God's friend?

Day 19: God's Love

The Father loves the Son and has placed everything in his hands. Whoever believes in the Son has eternal life, but whoever rejects the Son will not see life, for God's wrath remains on him (John 3:35,36).

Ultimate Word: *Read John 3:22-36*

Ultimate Encounter

Let's drop in on John the Baptist. Some of his disciples are complaining that he's losing his following—that this Jesus fellow is drawing a bigger box-office crowd.

But instead of hiring an ad agency or going for higher ratings, John simply explains that this is the way it has to be: "He must become greater; I must become less." He also uses a beautiful analogy, one that is found throughout the New Testament. He refers to Jesus as a groom and His followers (you and me) as His bride.

Think about that for a moment: God the Son wants a relationship with us that is so deep, so intimate, that it can be described as a groom who longs for his new bride. He wants to share *everything* He is with us. In fact, He's so in love that He values our lives more than His. That's why He was willing to go through the agony of the cross.

Talk about an intense, devoted love.

That's how special each one of us is to Him. That's the type of friendship God seeks with us; that's the type of intimacy we were created for; that's the type of unselfish love He wants to share. That's what we were originally created to enjoy. And that's what He yearns and cries out for us to accept.

Ultimate Action

Grasp this truth: You are a priceless person. You are a person set aside for God and His love. Your calling is far, far higher than the world's. You are royalty, and God demands that you treat yourself as such. Therefore, view yourself with that level of self-respect and self-confidence. Set your standards high.

Day 20: Living Water

Whoever drinks of this water will thirst again, but whoever drinks of the water that I shall give him will never thirst. But the water that I shall give him will become in him a fountain of water springing up into everlasting life (John 4:13,14 NKJV).

Ultimate Word: *Read John 4:1-26*

Ultimate Encounter

Samaritans were considered top-of-the-line, triple-A scuzzballs. In fact, the Jews hated them so much that they'd travel completely out of their way just to make sure their feet didn't touch Samaritan soil.

But not Jesus. He moves right on in. Not only does He enter their territory, but He actually strikes up a conversation with the "low-life vermin." Unheard of! But He figures scuzzballs need love, too. In fact, He said, "It is not the healthy who need a doctor, but the sick. I have not come to call the righteous, but sinners" (Mark 2:17).

Throughout her life, the Samaritan woman Jesus meets at the well has been trying to fill the emptiness inside her. She has tried desperately to quench the thirst in her soul. Like so many, she's certain she can fill that lonely emptiness by finding the perfect relationship, by finding "Mr. Right." But after six times at bat, she's not any closer to getting on base than when she started.

The only thing her attempts have done is to alienate her from the rest of the people. Let's face it, after six tries, this lady's got a reputation problem. (That's probably why she was facing the hot, midday sun instead of going to the well in the evening when things were cooler and everyone else was there.) The very thing she used to try to escape her loneliness actually made it worse.

Our attempts to create our own fulfillment usually fail. That's the trouble with sin or anything else we use to try to replace God. It simply will not last. In fact, it will eventually leave us thirstier than when we started. At first it may seem to satisfy, but eventually sin will always, *always* take more than it gives. It's like drinking salt water. For a moment it seems to do the trick. But in reality, the more salt water people drink, the thirstier they become. So they keep on drinking, getting thirstier and thirstier, drinking more, getting even thirstier, and so on until finally, well, you guessed it, they die. And you know what they die of? All the salt they have taken in demands too much water for their kidneys to keep functioning. So they die of dehydration. That's how sin works. It's a false satisfier that winds up killing people.

Jesus claims to be just the opposite. He says that He is *living water*. He says that all we have to do is drink of Him and we'll never be thirsty again; we'll never have that deep longing that just can't seem to be satisfied. In fact, He says that if we drink His water we'll have so much satisfaction, so much love, peace, and joy, that it'll actually be bubbling up from inside our souls and pouring over—as if we each had a private spring gurgling up inside us. It's a spring that's always available no matter what particular desert we may find ourselves wandering through.

Ultimate Action

Whenever temptation begins to take hold and a particular sin starts looking desirable, remind yourself that you've been given the power to resist it. In fact, memorize this verse: "Submit yourselves, then, to God. Resist the devil, and he will flee from you" (James 4:7).

Day 21: Real Satisfaction

"My food," said Jesus, "is to do the will of him who sent me and to finish his work. Do you not say, 'Four months more and then the harvest'? I tell you, open your eyes and look at the fields! They are ripe for harvest. Even now the reaper draws his wages, even now he harvests the crop for eternal life, so that the sower and the reaper may be glad together. Thus the saying 'One sows and another reaps' is true. I sent you to reap what you have not worked for. Others have done the hard work, and you have reaped the benefits of their labor" (John 4:34-38).

Ultimate Word: *Read John 4:27-42*

Ultimate Encounter

We're still at the well in Samaria. When the disciples return, they're pretty amazed to see Jesus chatting away with the Samaritan woman. It was bad enough she was a Samaritan, but the fact that she was a woman made it even worse. You see, the prejudice against women was pretty strong back then. In fact, the rabbis even had a saying that went, "It's better to burn the Law than give it to women."

Not nice.

Interestingly enough, despite all the knocks it gets from the world, Christianity has done more to free women from this second-rate citizen mentality than all of the current women's movements together. In fact, the New Testament teaches this radical concept: "There is neither Jew nor Greek, slave nor free, male nor female, for you are all one in Christ Jesus" (Galatians 3:28).

When the disciples returned and wanted to know what Jesus had eaten, He explained that His food, His real fulfillment, came from doing His Father's work. It's safe to say that helping this woman at the well was more satisfying to Jesus than any number of Big Macs He could have put away.

The same is true today. There is nothing more gratifying than helping someone understand what Christ has done and encouraging that person to accept His offer of salvation. There is nothing more satisfying than helping to save someone's life for eternity.

But today, in this age of "whoever dies with the most toys wins," it's sometimes hard to remember where real happiness lies. It's hard not to be tricked into thinking that satisfaction comes from material possessions. It's hard to remember that there's a deeper, more permanent joy—a joy that comes from friendship with God and from loving and serving His children.

Love and *service*—that's our real food, our real satisfaction.

Ultimate Action

If you're trying to decide what to do with your life, don't forget to check with God. See how He'd like you to be in service for Him. It's true that you may not get the house on the lake, the European vacations, or even that sporty Jaguar, but you'll be getting a deeper satisfaction—a satisfaction that the others, with only their toys, can never achieve.

Today, more than ever, the fields really are "ripe for harvest." There are millions who have never even heard the name of Jesus. There is an entire world out there (and in your own backyard) that is sick and hungry and generally beaten up. A world that is literally going to hell. The question is: *Does God want you to help share the good news of the gospel?*

It won't always be easy; it won't always be fun and games. But it will *always* be an adventure. And the benefits? The dividends are definitely out of this world.

ULTIMATE Wisdom!

Week Four

X

Encounter
Jesus'
eternal
teachings—
a timeless
treasure
chest
of wisdom
we just
can't
miss.

Day 22: New Life

No one puts a piece from a new garment on an old one; otherwise the new makes a tear, and also the piece that was taken out of the new does not match the old (Luke 5:36 NKJV).

Ultimate Word: *Read Luke 5:33-39*

Ultimate Encounter

The Pharisees and the teachers of the law are pretty perplexed by Jesus and His followers. One official questions Jesus about his followers' laid-back attitude: "John's disciples often fast and pray, and so do the disciples of the Pharisees, but yours go on eating and drinking."

In other words, "What's going on? These people who follow You are enjoying life way too much! Where's their commitment to religious traditions and legal requirements? Don't they know that good religious people give up food and drink twice a week as a sign of devotion to the law and a sign of mourning because the Messiah hasn't come to set us free?"

Jesus' response? "No one tears a patch from a new garment and sews it on an old one. If he does, he will have torn the new garment, and the patch from the new won't match the old."

Translation: "Give me a break! You're telling Me, the Creator of the Sabbath, what to do on the Sabbath? My disciples worship the one and only God—*Me!* My Father in heaven has sent the world its Messiah, His Son—*Me!* And

I'm leading My followers on a new, fresh way. The way of grace. So give up your rules and start following *My* truth."

Jesus points out the need for people to throw out the old life. It does no good to simply add Jesus to our lives, to receive Him and continue chasing after the world. We should be willing to let Him clear out the old and replace it with the new life He offers.

That's exactly what Matthew did. He left behind everything to follow Jesus. Matthew didn't try to add Jesus to his life like adding a patch to rotting jeans. Instead, he completely replaced his rags with a brand-new pair. If you receive Jesus, you don't add Him to your lives to fix it up. Instead, you let Him toss your old life away so there's room for a new one—His.

Ultimate Action

✔ Ask Jesus to help you break free from old ways of thinking and acting, from a lifestyle filled with envy, pride, anger, jealousy, lust, and confusion.

✔ Ask Jesus to show you a new way of living—a lifestyle filled with satisfaction, celebration, joy, unity, wholeness, and peace.

✔ Ask Jesus to take total control of your life.

Day 23: Team Jesus

When morning came, he called his disciples to him and chose twelve of them, whom he also designated apostles: Simon (whom he named Peter), his brother Andrew, James, John, Philip, Bartholomew, Matthew, Thomas, James son of Alphaeus, Simon who was called the Zealot, Judas son of James, and Judas Iscariot, who became a traitor (Luke 6:13-16).

Ultimate Word: *Read Luke 6:12-26*

Ultimate Encounter

Jesus ponders some important questions: Who will be His apostles? Who will be His inner circle of close friends that will spread the gospel after He leaves? Instead of relying on charts, figures, and computers, Jesus spends an entire night praying to the Father.

He names the twelve disciples. They're just ordinary men with different backgrounds. Some are even bitter enemies. (Matthew, the tax collector, is considered a traitor to his country, while Simon the Zealot belongs to an organization that wants to kill all traitors.) The twelve men make an interesting combination, but the love of Jesus breaks down all barriers and teaches them to work with one another and to love one another.

Jesus now begins His famous Sermon on the Mount, considered by many scholars to be history's greatest teaching. Our Savior starts off by saying how blessed we are if we're poor, hungry, weeping, and even hated because of Him. In fact, He says if we are insulted because of Him, "rejoice in that day and leap for joy, because great is [our] reward in heaven." In other words, if we're really letting Jesus be Lord, our rewards won't always come through outward situations. But we can have the peace, the love, and the joy of the Holy Spirit bubbling up and overflowing inside us, something that no amount of money can buy. All that, plus the eternal rewards in heaven. Kind of a two-for-one deal. Not bad. Not bad at all. In fact, it's terrific!

On the other hand, if we're still chasing after the world, its riches, its superficial happiness, and its fame, we may get what we want—but that's all. There'll be no eternal life and no inner peace. In fact, Jesus says such people will be unhappy. Not only that, but they will miss out on a super eternity. After their worldly pride and fun wears off, the things they valued will become totally worthless.

Remember how much we wanted something for Christmas when we were younger? Whatever we got was fun for a while....But as the weeks passed, we got bored and wanted something else. The same is still true, whether the coveted toy is a computer game, an expensive sports car, or diamonds and pearls.

Nothing can possibly fill that empty space in our hearts that was especially designed for God to fill—except God Himself.

Ultimate Action

✔ *Cling to the truth.* When the going gets rough in life and you feel the temptation of breaking away from Jesus and operating on your own strength, remember this truth: *God loves you and knows what He's doing.*

✔ *Stay on course.* If you've made the decision to follow God, rest assured that the trip will be incredible (if it hasn't been already). You'll go places you've never dreamed about; you'll see things you never imagined. Granted, you will go through rain, blizzards, and storms of various kinds, but as long as you stay under His protection, you'll make it big time. The storm will pass, life will get better, and you'll find complete fulfillment.

Day 24: Random Acts of Love

But love your enemies, and do good, and lend, expecting nothing in return; and your reward will be great, and you will be sons of the Most High; for He Himself is kind to ungrateful and evil men. Be merciful, just as your Father is merciful (Luke 6:35,36 NASB).

Ultimate Word: *Read Luke 6:27-38*

Ultimate Encounter

In the Sermon on the Mount, Jesus is speaking of love. Not the gushy sentimentality that people manufacture, package, and show on TV, but the firm, active, selfless love that can come only from God—

✔ a love for those who hate us

✔ a love that causes us to bless and even pray for those who mistreat us

✔ a love that is concerned for others

✔ a love that gives without expecting anything in return

Before Jesus came on the scene, the great religious saying of the time was, "Don't do anything to anybody that you wouldn't want them to do to you." But Jesus indicates that "not doing" to others is only the beginning.

We are to "do to others" what we want them to do for us. We are to become just as merciful as our Father.

We are not to pass judgment or condemn, but to forgive and pardon—then we'll be forgiven and pardoned.

If we give, it will be given back to us with interest. Incredible!

The previous thoughts show God's love. And if they all sound impossible to live by, you're right. Only God can live by them because only He has a love like that. But as we submit to Him, as we continue to allow Him to be the boss, we slowly find that we can begin to do those things—not because we have to, but because we want to.

Ultimate Action

Crack open your Bible and flip over to 1 John 3:16, which says, "This is how we know what love is: Jesus Christ laid down his life for us." Now read the rest of 3:16 and verses 17-24. Ask God to help you "love in truth and action." Pray something like this:

Lord, show me what I can do. Show me how to open my heart to the poor, the hungry, the broken. Show me how to overcome any bitterness in my heart. Teach me how to forgive. Let me see with Your eyes and love with Your heart. Amen.

Day 25: Way of the Wise

Why do you look at the speck of sawdust in your brother's eye and pay no attention to the plank in your own eye? How can you say to your brother, "Brother, let me take the speck out of your eye," when you yourself fail to see the plank in your own eye? You hypocrite, first take the plank out of your eye, and then you will see clearly to remove the speck from your brother's eye (Luke 6:41,42).

Ultimate Word: *Read Luke 6:39-49*

Ultimate Encounter

Jesus reminds us with a humorous illustration to get our acts together before we start trying to clean other people's lives: "Why do you look at the speck of sawdust in your brother's eye and pay no attention to the plank in your own eye?"

Jesus also says we act out what we are inside. If we're a lemon tree (if we haven't let Jesus come in and begin to change us), try as we might on our own to grow peaches, we'll grow lemons. Oh sure, we can fake it for a while and look as if we're growing peaches—you know, paint our fruit and glue some fuzz on the outside. We may even fool ourselves for a while. But as soon as someone takes a bite, he gets lemon (plus a mouthful of fuzz). On the other hand, a peach tree can only bear peaches. It can't help it. It doesn't strain or strive. The fruit just comes out that way.

Jesus also tells us to build our houses with firm foundations in Him, not like those who go for the quick payoff. Sand castles may look great and are a snap to build, but they're short-term investments. One rain or big wave, and it's all over. Jesus encourages us to build on His rock, His firm foundation—and with materials that will last.

Jesus had much to say and much to do while He was here on earth. There were so many things that the Creator had to say about living in His creation. In fact, after the apostle John wrote an entire book on Jesus, he ended with this statement: "Jesus did many other things as well. If every one of them were written down, I suppose that even the whole world would not have room for the books that would be written" (John 21:25). This may also have been the case for Luke. He had so much to record that he had to abruptly end one point and begin another to get it all in his book.

The bottom line is that Jesus wants us to know the truth. He wants us to understand that real satisfaction can't be found in girlfriends, boyfriends, money, popularity, or beefed-up brain cells. Our most urgent need isn't the latest computer game or a date to the prom. What we really need is the life that only God can give. What's more, we need to draw upon nourishment from Christ. We need the strength God gives through His Word, prayer, fellowship, and worship.

Ultimate Action

✔ *Examine your attitude.* Do others see the truth in you? Do they know you follow Christ? Do they know you're full of the life, joy, and peace that only God can give?

✔ *Build on the Rock.* If you're depending on anything or anyone other than Jesus Christ to give you real life and ultimate fulfillment, know that your life is stuck in sand—sinking sand. *Jesus Christ is the only solid foundation.* Make a change. Seek Him; trust Him.

Day 26: Salt and Light

You are the salt of the earth; but if the salt has become tasteless, how will it be made salty again? It is good for nothing anymore, except to be thrown out and trampled under foot by men. You are the light of the world. A city set on a hill cannot be hidden (Matthew 5:13,14 NASB).

Ultimate Word: *Matthew 5:12-16*

Ultimate Encounter

"You are the salt of the earth," Jesus tells His followers. "You are the light of the world." What an amazing picture. What an astonishing way to describe a Christian. And Jesus wants His disciples to understand that following Him means standing up, stepping out, and making a positive, life-changing impact on this mixed-up planet. We can't just sit still and keep quiet. "But if the salt loses its saltiness, how can it be made salty again?" Jesus warns. "It is no longer good for anything."

Do you have the courage to stand up for Jesus Christ in the face of opposition? Or do you find your faith being trampled by your friends? Does your light shine among others? Or are you more like a burned-out light bulb?

Remember Cassie Bernall, the student at Columbine High School in Colorado who was shot because she stood up for Christ? She was willing to lay down her life for her Savior. Are we willing to lay down our precious reputations?

Too many of us think that because we're Christians, we're supposed to be accepting about everything. That's not true. Jesus *never* asks us to accept anything that goes against His holy Word. In fact, He wants us to speak up for what's right! In short, He wants us to *live and speak our faith*.

Ultimate Action

✔ *Stand strong for Jesus.* When people look at your life, make sure they see someone with a sincere heart—not a guy or gal hiding behind a mask.

✔ *Be willing to get involved.* Keep in mind that even if you're not a hotshot quarterback or the prom queen you're definitely a champion if you've taken the gutsy, tough steps that help make a difference in someone's life.

✔ *Be compassionate but honest.* Understand that, as a Christian, if you tell your friends that something is wrong because the Bible calls it sin, you're not being judgmental, you're merely repeating what the Bible says. If someone is eating poison and killing him- or herself, there's more love in speaking up and sounding a warning than keeping quiet and watching that person eat. How much more important is it to share God's truths and the salvation He offers through Jesus!

Day 27: Why Worry?

Therefore do not worry, saying, "What shall we eat?" or "What shall we drink?" or "What shall we wear?"...Your heavenly Father knows that you need all these things. But seek first the kingdom of God and His righteousness, and all these things shall be added to you (Matthew 6:31-33 NKJV).

Ultimate Word: *Read Matthew 6:25-34*

Ultimate Encounter

Stomachs have churned with worry since the beginning of time. And it was no different in Jesus' day. Take His friend Martha, for example. Let's skip over to Luke 10:40-42 and check out this lady with a bad case of the worries:

> But Martha was distracted by all the preparations that had to be made. She came to him and asked, "Lord, don't you care that my sister has left me to do the work by myself? Tell her to help me!"

> "Martha, Martha," the Lord answered, "you are worried and upset about many things, but only one thing is needed. Mary has chosen what is better, and it will not be taken away from her."

Ouch! Martha's tension turns to worry, and Jesus gives her a dose of reality.

Now let's get back to the action of the Sermon on the Mount and eavesdrop on Christ's soothing solution about worry.

"But seek first the kingdom of God and His righteousness, and all these things shall be added to you" (Matthew 6:33 NKJV). This is Jesus' answer to hearts that are bursting with worry. Look to Him first, that's the important thing. Jesus wants to have first place in our hearts, and He'll take care of the rest.

A life without worries—impossible, right? Wrong. You can rest assured that God cares for you: "The LORD is good, a refuge in times of trouble. He cares for those who trust in him" (Nahum 1:7). And you can rest assured that God is in control: "Be still, and know that I am God; I will be exalted among the nations, I will be exalted in the earth" (Psalm 46:10).

Ultimate Action

Whenever you find yourself stressing out about something, stop and pray. Focus on God, and He'll always provide the answer—*always*. It may not be the answer you're expecting or within your own time frame, but His response will always be for the best—*always*.

Day 28: Narrow Gates

Enter through the narrow gate. For wide is the gate and broad is the road that leads to destruction, and many enter through it. But small is the gate and narrow the road that leads to life, and only a few find it (Matthew 7:13,14).

Ultimate Word: *Read Matthew 7:13-23*

Ultimate Encounter

Jesus' Sermon on the Mount teaches the values of His kingdom, and these puzzle the Jewish people. Consider this warning from Matthew 6:24: "No one can serve two masters. Either he will hate the one and love the other, or he will be devoted to the one and despise the other. You cannot serve both God and Money." Essentially, Christ is telling the crowds that wealth, the law, and the values of this world that people hold so high won't get them into the kingdom. In fact, relying only on these things "is the road that leads to destruction."

Emotions are definitely heating up. Everything Jesus says points in a direction that most people aren't willing to go. His commands don't just forbid murder and adultery; Jesus says they include even hatred and lust (the inner attitudes behind the actions).

Then He hits the crowd right between the eyes: "For I tell you that unless your righteousness surpasses that of the Pharisees and the teachers of the law, you will certainly not enter the kingdom of heaven" (Matthew 5:20). Add to that this zinger: "Not everyone who says to me, 'Lord, Lord,' will enter the kingdom of heaven, but only he who does the will of my Father who is in heaven" (Matthew 7:21).

Is Jesus holding up a standard that is too high for anyone to attain? Not on your life. His point is this: It's not a matter of human ability. He's the one who gives us the power not to sin. And if we mess up, He'll *always* forgive us and help us start over again.

For most of us, heaven is a lifetime away, so we're tempted to look to the easy route. Many people point us toward this easy, wide road: kids at school, much of the media, teachers, and sometimes even parents. Unfortunately, the easy route doesn't head in the right direction.

But other people point us toward the right road—the narrow one: parents, pastors, youth leaders, caring friends, and, of course, Jesus.

Which kingdom will we finally reach? God has made it clear which one He wants us to choose. Now it's our turn to make the choice.

Ultimate Action

✔ *Confess.* Are there sins you need to talk to Jesus about? Coming clean is crucial to building a deeper relationship with Him.

✔ *Submit.* If Jesus Christ is truly your Lord, that means He's your Master. Make an effort to obey Him and to rely on His strength. (See Psalm 28:7.)

✔ *Dedicate.* Knowing God is a lifelong process. Commit to spending time with Him every day. Make knowing Him your top priority.

ULTIMATE
Commitment!

Week Five

X

Christic
freely
offers
abundant,
eternal
life—but
only to
those who
freely
commit
their
lives
to Him.

Day 29: Simple Faith

"Assuredly, I say to you, I have not found such great faith, not even in Israel! And I say to you that many will come from east and west, and sit down with Abraham, Isaac, and Jacob in the kingdom of heaven. But the sons of the kingdom will be cast out into outer darkness. There will be weeping and gnashing of teeth." Then Jesus said to the centurion, "Go your way; and as you have believed, so let it be done for you." And his servant was healed that same hour (Matthew 8:10-13 NKJV).

Ultimate Word: *Read Matthew 8:5-13*

Ultimate Encounter

A lot of people think that healings back in Jesus' day (and even in our day) are basically mind over matter. A person wants to be healed so badly or gets so worked up emotionally that his or her mind makes the healing happen.

But nothing could be further from the truth when Jesus healed the centurion's servant. Let's face it, the poor guy doesn't even know what's going on. Here he lies, sick and dying in Capernaum, when all the way over at Cana Jesus says he's healed.

The servant isn't doing anything; he doesn't hear anything; he isn't at some "faith rally" getting all worked up and screaming, "I believe, I believe." He just lies there—dying—until Jesus says, "He will live."

This is the only time in the entire New Testament that Jesus marvels at someone's faith. He turns to the crowd and says, "I tell you, I have not found such great faith even in Israel" (see Luke 7:9).

Jesus was on a mission. From sunup to sundown He healed the sick, cast demons out of people, and proclaimed that the day of liberation had come. Absolute freedom from fear, from worry, from bad thoughts, from bad actions, from bitterness, from grief...from chasing after what the world claims is so important.

The Divine walked among the destructive. And with Him came restored hope and healed hearts. Through His miracles He told the world, "I am God, and I have brought you eternal life."

The only thing He asks in return is that we have simple, absolute faith. And that's exactly what He found with this Roman centurion: *God says it, I believe it, that settles it.*

Ultimate Action

✔ *Simple faith is not something we can manufacture.* We can't buy it at the local Christian bookstore. Such faith can only come from God as we continue to know Him better, to fall deeper in love with Him, and to yield to Him.

✔ *Understand that miracles are not mind over matter.* They are God over matter. Sometimes they happen; sometimes they don't. But the point is they come from God—not people.

✔ *God doesn't need our help to perform His miracles.* He doesn't need us to get all worked up and emotionally hyped. He only wants us to trust and and obey. The rest is up to Him.

Day 30: Out of the Coffin

Then he went up and touched the coffin, and those carrying it stood still. He said, "Young man, I say to you, get up!" The dead man sat up and began to talk, and Jesus gave him back to his mother (Luke 7:14,15).

Ultimate Word: *Read Luke 7:11-17*

Ultimate Encounter

A crowd follows Jesus as He travels to Nain, about a day's walk from Capernaum. As they approach the city gate, Jesus and the crowd are met by another crowd heading for the local graveyard.

The funeral is a loud affair. Professional mourners, a custom in that day, have been hired, and they lead the procession clanging cymbals, playing flutes, and wailing. The mother walks alone behind this sad group. The coffin containing her dead son follows behind.

A mother losing her only child is a painful thought. What's more, the woman's husband is also dead. This means she's now completely alone. Whom will she turn to? How will she survive? Who can possibly comfort her now? Her heartache and misery must be unbearable.

As Jesus' eyes meet hers, He is filled with compassion. It's comforting to know that as we go through heartache, pain, and suffering, Jesus is right there by our side, feeling every tear, every ache, every bit of sorrow.

But in this instance, Jesus does more than feel sad. He stops the procession and exercises His authority over death. And something amazing happens. The young man comes back to life and crawls out of the coffin!

Today, thousands of people who are trying Eastern philosophies and the "you can improve yourself" religions overlook the fact that Jesus is the only teacher who has authority over death. Other philosophers may have catchy slogans or ideas, but when it comes to death they're powerless. Yet in just three years Jesus exercises His power over death at least four times!

It's interesting that in Luke 7:14 Jesus doesn't say, "In the name of God, arise." Instead He proves once again that He is God with the words, "I say to you, get up!" The man rises up and begins talking. All are amazed at Jesus' display of power, and they begin calling Him a prophet. (Well, at least they're getting close.)

Ultimate Action

Jesus wants complete authority over your life. He wants your complete trust. Take some time to evaluate your relationship with Jesus. Is there anything holding you back from giving Him complete authority? Spend time in prayer, asking Him to help you let go of it.

Day 31: Selfless Servant

Jesus said to him, "Rise, take up your bed and walk." And immediately the man was made well, took up his bed, and walked. (John 5:8,9 NKJV).

Ultimate Word: *Read John 5:1-15*

Ultimate Encounter

We're in Jerusalem by a special healing pool. According to the Bible, "An angel of the Lord went down at certain seasons...and stirred up the water; whoever then first, after the stirring up of the water, stepped in was made well" (John 5:4 NASB). So here's this guy, unable to walk, crowded in with the rest of the city's suffering—his only goal to scratch and claw to be the first into the pool to get healed. And to top it off he's been doing this for 38 years and still hasn't succeeded! Life must be pretty miserable for him!

In some ways, the life of the sick man at the pool isn't too different from our lives. We may not have a healing pool to fight and claw to get to, but in this pressure-cooker world of ours we certainly have enough other struggles: "I've got to get better grades to get into a better school, to get a better job, to get better money, to have a better life." Or, for those who think in short-range terms: "I've got to get that parking spot before he does!"

Whatever our goals, we are living in a world full of competition. It's a hard, vicious, exhausting game. Forget about being a superstar. For most of us, just trying to get on the scoreboard is tough enough. But the good news is we don't have to score points—we don't even have to play the game!

"But if I don't score more points than what's-his-face, then what's-his-face'll get all the prizes!"

He might. But so will you—*if you put Christ first.* "But seek first his kingdom and his righteousness, and all these things will be given to you as well" (Matthew 6:33). That doesn't mean you'll breeze through your SATs, cruise into Harvard, become president of IBM, and make your first million by age 20. But putting Christ first does mean He will pick *you* out of the crowd (just as He did the lame man) and give you the wholeness and happiness you *really* want. If being rich will do it, then rich you'll probably be. But chances are, He'll be giving you a deeper and more lasting happiness, one that most billionaires will never have.

Bottom line: You don't have to claw your way to the top. All you have to do is obey Jesus. You have His Word on it.

Ultimate Action

While the rest of the world is kicking and fighting and scrambling, all you need to do is rest in the Lord. Refuse to be sucked into that hectic, frenzied, me-first thinking. Make your priority seeking Jesus and obeying Him; after that, the *real* prizes will come. He'll make sure of it.

Day 32: Ultimate Life-Giver

Jesus said to them, "My Father is always at his work to this very day, and I, too, am working." For this reason the Jews tried all the harder to kill him; not only was he breaking the Sabbath, but he was even calling God his own Father, making himself equal with God (John 5:17,18).

Ultimate Word: *Read John 5:16-30*

Ultimate Encounter

Remember the guy Jesus healed at the Sheep Gate, or Bethesda, pool? Now the religious hotshots are complaining that Jesus by healing him broke the Sabbath. Jesus blows them away by saying, "Hey look, My Father does good on the Sabbath, so why shouldn't I? If it's good enough for God, it's good enough for Me."

This raises everyone's blood pressure a few dozen points because once again Jesus is making Himself equal with God. And just to make sure there's no mistake about it, He goes on to state a few other spectacular claims:

> ✔ The Father shows Jesus everything He does (John 5:20).

> ✔ Jesus can give eternal life to whomever He wants (verse 21).

> ✔ The Father has given all authority of judging the world to Jesus (verse 22).

✔ Anyone who hears and believes Jesus will live forever (verse 24).

Now these are pretty radical claims. No wonder the people are trying to kill Him! But the greatest claim comes in verse 23: "He who does not honor the Son does not honor the Father, who sent Him."

Quite a statement—and a pretty clear answer to the following argument: "Hey, don't get me wrong. I believe in a god out there somewhere. I mean, I'm no atheist or anything like that. I just don't buy all this Jesus stuff." That may be so, but the problem is that we can't have one without the other. They're interconnected. The only way we can honor God is if we honor His Son. In other words:

If we reject Jesus, we reject God.

If we accept Jesus, we accept God.

God gives us no other alternative.

Ultimate Action

Spend some time in prayer, talking to God:

Forgive me for the times that I've doubted You and Your authority. Give me the strength to trust, honor, and obey. Fill me with Your Holy Spirit and lead me to a deeper faith in You. Amen.

Day 33: Religion v. Relationship

But the witness which I have is greater than that of John; for the works which the Father has given Me to accomplish, the very works that I do, bear witness of Me, that the Father has sent Me. And the Father who sent Me, He has borne witness of Me. You have neither heard His voice at any time, nor seen His form. And you do not have His word abiding in you, for you do not believe Him whom He sent (John 5:36-38 NASB).

Ultimate Word: *Read John 5:31-47*

Ultimate Encounter

Some people will do anything they can *not* to surrender their life to Christ, even if it means becoming "Christians." Instead of quietly seeking Jesus with a sincere heart that says, "Whatever You want, it's Yours," they get involved in "works" so they can give Him just what they want to give. But today's Scripture passage says that's not enough.

In essence, this is what's happening in this section of John's account. All of these scholars have been carefully studying God's Word and the writings of Moses. By doing all of this religious work they think they're getting eternal life. But Jesus flat out says, "No way. All these things testify about Me and speak about Me—but they are not Me. And the Me part, that personal relationship with Me, that's what's going to save you; that's where real life is."

The same is true today. We can get so caught up in all of the religious things to say and do that we forget the one person everything points to—Jesus! Or, worse yet, we can end up using our "works" as an excuse not to get real with Him, to prevent Him from really touching our hearts. But the energized, overflowing life Jesus is always talking about comes from Him. It does not come from Bible studies; it does not come from Sunday school, youth group, choir practice, or sacrificial service to others. It doesn't even come from a perfect church attendance!

Ultimate Action

God doesn't want just your sacrifice. He wants your love. God doesn't want just your works. He wants your heart, also.

✔ Ask the Lord to help you learn how to worship Him. Tell Him that you really want to focus on Him and deepen your faith.

✔ Ask Jesus to help you make knowing Him *the priority* in your life.

Day 34: Obedience

When Jesus looked up and saw a great crowd coming toward him, he said to Philip, "Where shall we buy bread for these people to eat?"... Jesus then took the loaves, gave thanks, and distributed to those who were seated as much as they wanted. He did the same with the fish. When they had all had enough to eat, he said to his disciples, "Gather the pieces that are left over. Let nothing be wasted" (John 6:5,11,12).

Ultimate Word: *Read John 6:1-14*

Ultimate Encounter

A hefty crowd is starting to follow Jesus. He's been pretty busy in the miracle department and so far He's batting 1,000—a perfect score. So you'd think His question to the disciples about how to feed all the people wouldn't have been too tough to answer. Let's take a look at three responses to this question.

Philip: Like so many of us, Philip forgets what Jesus has done in the past. He forgets how much the Lord wants to bless us. Instead he looks at the situation and panics, basically saying: "Even if we scraped up eight months' wages, we couldn't feed this mob!"...O.K., thanks for sharing, Phil.

Andrew: Then there's Andrew, doing what he does best—bringing people to Jesus. Remember how he ran out and brought his brother, Peter, to Christ? This time, he's bringing a little boy with a few loaves of bread and a couple of fish. He's not sure how—or even if—but there's something inside him that figures Jesus might be able to pull this one off. It's as if there's this tiny little kernel of faith. Still, his question, "But how far will they go?" makes it pretty clear that he's not totally sold.

Little boy: Finally, there's the little boy. Now, it's a safe guess that the bread and fish are for his lunch, and they aren't much. The loaves are small and so are the fish. (In fact, some scholars today believe the fish were pickled and about the size of sardines.) But instead of hoarding the food, he volunteers to give it away. He trusts Jesus enough to give Him all that he has. And the result? Five thousand men (not to mention all the women and children) ate as much as they wanted, leaving twelve baskets full of leftovers! Not a bad return for the boy's investment.

Ultimate Action

✔ *Christ wants you to go for broke.* Just like the little boy in today's passage, put everything you have into Christ's hands. It's certainly not mandatory. You can hold back and make sure you have enough for yourself—and then, maybe, give Him a little of the leftovers. But look at the excitement and joy the boy would have missed if he had made that choice. Think of the selfish, boring day he would have had. Then think of the excitement that lies ahead for you if *you* put everything into Christ's hands!

✔ *Trust and give.* Look around you at all the selfish, boring lives of Christians who give God a little but refuse to trust Him all the way. It takes courage to trust God—to give Him all that you have. But it's like any other investment: The more you give, the more you receive. And by giving Him more and more of your life, you'll get more and more of His all-powerful life. Not a bad trade.

Day 35: Walkin' on Water

When they had rowed three or three and a half miles, they saw Jesus approaching the boat, walking on the water; and they were terrified. But he said to them, "It is I; don't be afraid." Then they were willing to take him into the boat, and immediately the boat reached the shore where they were heading (John 6:19-21).

Ultimate Word: *Read John 6:15-21*

Ultimate Encounter

Today's passage takes place right after Jesus fed the multitude with the boy's loaves and fish. When the people realize the miracle Jesus performed, they want to make Him king—and they are willing to take Him by force to do so. One of the reasons for this is that for years the Jews have been forced to live under Roman rule. So you can understand why, after seeing all His miracles, the Jews think they can use Jesus to do a little Roman-bashing.

But Jesus will not be manipulated. God wants to give the people overflowing life, but on His terms. He wants to save these people—but He wants to save them from Satan's clutches, not from the Romans. He wants to give them what they really need, not what they want.

So what does Jesus do when they try to force Him to play by their rules? He just sort of…disappears.

How often does He do that in our lives? When we try to force God to do something our way, how often does He seem to bow out? But Jesus is never far away.

And then the scene shifts to the disciples and the terrible time they're having....

It's been only a short while since the miracle with the bread and fish, yet already the disciples are having a rough time. They're in the middle of a storm, three and a half miles from shore, in the dead of night. Suddenly, they see Jesus walking on the water toward them. Their response? Not exactly a 10 on the Richter scale of faith. At this point, they should be saying, "Lord, once again we see You're who You claim to be. Thank You for coming to save us!" Instead, they freak. But Jesus' words calm and quiet them: "It is I; don't be afraid" (John 6:20).

The same Jesus who walked out on the people trying to manipulate Him, walked in on His disciples who really needed Him.

Ultimate Action

✔ *Know that Christ's plans are best.* Even though Jesus is always with you, He doesn't conform to what you want. He always wants what's best for you. So, the next time you try to manipulate and con God into letting you have your own narrow-minded way, don't be too surprised if, suddenly, in those particular situations, He refuses to compromise.

✔ *Know that Christ is your protector.* Take comfort in this truth the next time you're frightened or confused about something. Jesus isn't there to tell you you're a jerk for getting caught in a storm. He's not there to yell at you for having so little faith. Instead, He's always there to watch over you, to encourage you, to ease your fears. He is always there, willing to climb into your boat and weather the storm with you.

ULTIMATE Freedom!

Week Six

X

Christr
wants to
develop
in us a
particular
attitude,
one in
which our
arms are
stretched
out to Him,
seeking His
guidance.

Day 36: Believe in Me

Jesus answered and said to them, "This is the work of God, that you believe in Him whom He has sent" (John 6:29 NASB).

Ultimate Word: *Read John 6:22-29*

Ultimate Encounter

The morning after the loaves and fish miracle, the crowd starts looking for Jesus. They know the disciples left the night before without Him. They know there were no other boats available, so they're having a bit of a problem figuring out exactly how He slipped past them.

When they finally do catch up, Jesus points out that they really didn't search for Him because of the miracles—they came because they ate the bread He'd provided and were filled. Then He explains that even though they were satisfied by the bread, they shouldn't be so concerned about physical food, which spoils. He has a different type of food—a food for the soul that satisfies a deeper hunger, a food that satisfies the hunger for love, truth, and fulfillment. And, most important, He points out that it is a food only He can provide.

The people immediately want to know what they can do to earn this love, this fulfilled life. In short, they want to know what they can do to earn God's favor. Jesus' answer couldn't be simpler: "Believe in Me."

Too often, people who encountered Christ couldn't see past the here and now—past the physical world. Too often, they missed the supernatural—the One who extended His hands and said, "Come follow Me...to eternity!"

The same is true today. Sometimes Christians spend too much time dining at "Café World," filling themselves with the distractions of the moment: material gain, popularity, and money. But Jesus wants more for us. He wants to satisfy our deepest hungers. He wants to dine with us at His eternal table.

And He has given us His invitation: "Believe in Me."

Ultimate Action

Evaluate your motives. Are you a Christian because it's the family thing to do? Do you attend youth group because that's where all your friends hang out?

What are you hungry for? Spend some time in prayer, asking Jesus to help you hunger for Him, not the world. Ask Him to quench your thirst with peace, joy, fulfillment, happiness, spiritual wisdom, and strength.

Day 37: Bread of Life

Jesus said to them, "I tell you the truth, it is not Moses who has given you the bread from heaven, but it is my Father who gives you the true bread from heaven. For the bread of God is he who comes down from heaven and gives life to the world" (John 6:32,33).

Ultimate Word: *Read John 6:30-58*

Ultimate Encounter

The conversation between Jesus and His disciples is starting to get interesting...not to mention confusing. Jesus had just explained what everyone must do to earn God's favor: "Believe in me." So far, the disciples are tracking with Him. "Fine," they say. "If you want us to believe in You, then show us a sign." (As if He hadn't shown them enough already!) "You've fed us only one meal; Moses gave our ancestors bread from heaven everyday for forty years. Top that."

Not only can Jesus top it—He says *He is it.*

"I am the bread of life. He who comes to Me will never go hungry, and he who believes in me will never be thirsty.... For I have come down from heaven not to do my will but to do the will of him who sent me" (John 6:35,38, emphasis added).

Suddenly, mouths drop open. "Isn't this guy the son of Joseph, whose father and mother we know?" the people grumble. "How can he now say, 'I came down from heaven'?"

Jesus wasn't about to force anyone to believe that He is the Messiah. That's not the way He works. Instead, He told the crowd to relax, then pointed out a truth: "Everyone who listens to the Father and learns from him comes to me....I am the living bread that came down from heaven. If anyone eats of this bread, he will live forever" (John 6:45,51).

The same is true today. If people are sincerely looking for truth, then Jesus will reveal Himself. And those who find Him, find eternal life with God. Those who reject Him, reject the Father (and heaven). What's more, if we've given ourselves to Jesus, in His name we can have complete and total authority over Satan—in anything, including bad habits, sin, fear of witnessing, sickness, and demonic activity!

But remember, Satan is a liar, and He'll use every lie he can dream up to make us think we haven't won. He wants us to believe nothing has changed inside us, that we can't have victory over certain areas in our lives. But it won't work if we draw close to Jesus and turn to Him in times of trouble.

Ultimate Action

Don't give in; don't dine with the devil. Claim the victory and eat the Living Bread. Seek the Savior, then trust Him. Pray: "Lord Jesus, break my stubborn will. Help me hunger for the Living Bread. Open my eyes and heart to You. Amen."

Day 38: Communion

Jesus said to them, "I tell you the truth, unless you eat the flesh of the Son of Man and drink his blood, you have no life in you. Whoever eats my flesh and drinks my blood has eternal life, and I will raise him up at the last day. For my flesh is real food and my blood is real drink" (John 6:53-55).

Ultimate Word: *Read John 6:41-59*

Ultimate Encounter

"Eat my flesh; drink my blood."

This is one of the most important instructions to Christians in the entire Bible. Unfortunately, many people have completely misunderstood it. In fact, some have even accused Christians of being cannibals! What they don't understand is that this is the number-one ingredient in the life of any believer in Jesus Christ.

As humans, we are made up of amino acids, water, minerals, and so forth. For the most part, we cannot manufacture these ingredients on our own. We need to take them into our system. We need to consume them. If we do, we live. If we don't, we die. For instance, if we didn't drink water or liquids, our bodies would cease to function.

The same is true with our spiritual nature. We cannot manufacture spiritual ingredients on our own. To survive spiritually, we have to consume spiritual food. And that's what Jesus claims to be.

Our spiritual food is Jesus Christ. In other words, we have to *spiritually* eat Him. We have to digest Him and allow Him to become incorporated into our spiritual beings. He wants to draw so close and love us so deeply that He starts to become a part of us. It is that oneness that gives us overwhelming love, peace, and joy. It is that oneness that gives us the abundant life He keeps promising.

But if we refuse, if we don't eat His body and drink His blood as He commanded, if we refuse to commune and have fellowship with Him, the only thing waiting for us is spiritual starvation.

And with starvation comes death.

Ultimate Action

Stop settling for fast food—a quick prayer here and a Bible verse there—and sit down to a gourmet meal. Have a serious quiet time each morning or night. Beginning today, carve out some time each day to spend at least 15 minutes in the Word and prayer. Steadily increase your time with God.

Day 39: Consumed by Christ

On hearing [Jesus' teaching that He is "the living bread" and anyone who eats of this bread will live forever], many of his disciples said, "This is a hard teaching. Who can accept it?" Aware that his disciples were grumbling about this, Jesus said to them, "Does this offend you? What if you see the Son of Man ascend to where he was before! The Spirit gives life; the flesh counts for nothing. The words I have spoken to you are spirit and they are life. Yet there are some of you who do not believe" (John 6:60-64).

Ultimate Word: *Read John 6:60-71*

Ultimate Encounter

This is one of the greatest tests in Jesus' life. The crowds are growing. They're following Him wherever He goes. In fact, as we've already read, they even want to make Him king.

Talk about an opportunity! By just keeping His mouth shut, Jesus can have all the power, fame, and riches that others only dream about. By not telling the whole truth, by candy-coating it ever so slightly, He can have everybody following Him.

But Jesus is not after numbers. He's not interested in quantity; He's interested in quality. If it means only twelve men and some women following Him then so be it—but those few will be entirely committed. They won't be fence-sitters. They won't be people who are "kind of into Jesus" and "kind of into the world." They will be people totally sold out to Him.

This is what God expects today. He doesn't ask us to add a little of Himself into our lives; He asks to *become* our lives. He's not interested in people who dabble in Jesus; He's interested in people who *live* Him.

Check out Revelation 3:15,16: "I know your deeds, that you are neither cold nor hot. I wish you were either one or the other! So, because you are lukewarm—neither hot nor cold—I am about to spit you out of my mouth."

Jesus is not interested in people who play church. He's interested in people who are the church—people who are a living, breathing, loving part of His body. He wants people who are totally committed to Him.

Ultimate Action

If you're not interested in putting Jesus first, then maybe you're just fooling yourself. Maybe you're like the multitudes that were just hanging around for another free meal (or because that's where their friends were, or because they wanted to use Jesus for selfish motives). If that's the case, then maybe you should move on and stop playing church.

There's just one little problem. Simon Peter saw it, and it's just as true today as it was then: "Lord, to whom shall we go? You have the words of eternal life" (John 6:68).

Day 40: Freed from Legalism

Why are you angry with me for healing the whole man on the Sabbath? Stop judging by mere appearances, and make a right judgment (John 7:23,24).

Ultimate Word: *Read John 7:1-24*

Ultimate Encounter

The "Feast of Tabernacles" is coming up. This is a big, eight-day celebration in mid-October that is similar to our Thanksgiving. Anybody who's anybody tries to make it to Jerusalem for the good times.

So Jesus' brothers begin taunting Him: "Hey listen, Mr. Miracles. You think You're so special, then head on up to Jerusalem. Let everyone see what a big man You are with Your fancy magic tricks!" But just as before, Jesus isn't letting anyone force His hand. He's going, all right, but on His terms—not at the beginning, but later on when the party's in full swing.

By the time He arrives (incognito), He's already the talk of the town (or whisper of the town, since everybody's afraid to speak up because of the religious leaders). Some of the people are saying He's a "good man,"others are saying He's a trickster. No one is paying attention to who He says He is. (Is this any different today?)

About halfway through the festival, Jesus finally makes His appearance at the temple court (the very center of the Jewish religion). He begins to teach, and the bigwigs are pretty impressed. They want to know how He got so smart without attending Jerusalem U.

"My teaching is not my own," Jesus says. "It comes from him who sent me!" (John 7:16) Figuring this is going to create the usual problems, He again tells them to check out His credentials. Basically He says, "Ask God—see if I'm for real. And if I am for real, then ask yourself why you're trying to kill Me."

"You're crackers!" they shout. "No one's trying to kill You!"

Knowing better, Jesus continues: "I did one miracle on the Sabbath (the healing of the man at the pool), and you're all hot and bothered. Everyone's bent out of shape because I helped some poor guy who'd been suffering for years. Yet you circumcise babies on this very same day! Tell Me, what's more important—following some religious ritual of circumcision or loving and healing a human being?

"Stop being so legalistic!" He continues. "Look at the whole picture. Don't judge by outward appearances. Get all the facts. If you're going to judge, at least get help from the final authority—God!"

Do either of these statements describe you? "I'm all talk and no action." "I'm trying to work my way into heaven"? If so, it's time to find real faith, and the only way to do that is to hook up with the real faith giver—Jesus Christ:

✔ Trust that Jesus is the Messiah....

✔ Believe in Him....

✔ Study His Word—the Holy Scriptures....

✔ Obey His commands....

Ultimate Action

✔ *Make sure your heart is sincere.* Do you truly believe that Christ is who He says He is? Do a little soul searching...and ask God to help you. Ask Jesus to help you work through any doubts you have. Also, talk about your concerns with your parents or pastor or youth worker.

✔ *Put your faith into practice.* Do what God says. Joining a Bible-study group and having an accountability partner is a great help.

Day 41: Unplugging Pride

Then Jesus...cried out, "Yes, you know me, and you know where I am from. I am not here on my own, but he who sent me is true. You do not know him, but I know him because I am from him and he sent me." At this they tried to seize him, but no one laid a hand on him (John 7:28-30).

Ultimate Word: *Read John 7:25-36*

Ultimate Encounter

The people finally catch on that Jesus is the one everyone's been talking about. This is no great feat, but to actually believe He's Christ—well now, that's another thing all together.

"Besides," they say, "everybody knows where this guy's from; when the Christ comes no one will know where He's from." (Not exactly true. Most everyone knew the prophecy in Micah 5:2 that said the Christ would be born in Bethlehem.)

But right now Jesus isn't particularly interested in going through His life history; He's interested in preaching the truth and helping people. Unfortunately, people like help, but the "truth" part, especially when it's directed at their personal lives, can make them a little irritable. Look how they try to seize Jesus when He points out that they don't really know God. But because "his time had not yet come," they can't touch Him (see John 7:30).

The same thing happens when the Pharisees send out the guards to arrest Him. For some reason they don't grab Jesus. Instead, they wind up listening to Him.

But the good times won't last forever. Jesus explains that pretty soon He'll be taking off and heading back to "the one who sent me" (verse 33).

It's often hard being confronted with the truth about our less-than-perfect motives and behaviors. Someone holds up a mirror and we cringe. Too often pride keeps us from accepting the truth. That's how it was in biblical times, and that's exactly how it is today.

Ultimate Action

Ask Jesus to search your heart and to help you pinpoint *specific* sins that are holding you back from an obedient relationship with Him. Ask God to do a deep work in your soul. Allow Him to examine every area of your life, and let Him conform your heart to Jesus'.

Day 42: Living Springs

If anyone is thirsty, let him come to me and drink. Whoever believes in me, as the Scripture has said, streams of living water will flow from within him (John 7:37,38).

Ultimate Word: *Read John 7:37-53*

Ultimate Encounter

As part of the ceremony of the Feast of Tabernacles, the priest pours water on the temple altar while the people shout praises to God. It's quite a spectacle and designed in part to thank God for His life-giving gift of water.

Everybody's into this celebration when suddenly Jesus stands up and shouts, "If anyone is thirsty, let him come to me and drink." No doubt that puts a little crimp in the ceremony. Not only is Jesus interrupting the action, but He's claiming to be the source of something far more real and far more important than what they're currently praising God for.

Notice again how much the Pharisees hate Jesus. But why? It's got to be more than the fact that He's interrupted a ceremony or two. If they think He's a madman, why not just have Him committed? If they think He's a con artist, just expose Him and lock Him up. And if He really is who He says He is, then they should drop to their knees in joy. After all, if this is the one they've been waiting for all these years, it should be "Hallelujah Chorus" time!

Unfortunately, the same reason the Pharisees hated Jesus back then is the same reason a lot of people hate and refuse Him today. It has nothing to do with clear thinking or logic. It doesn't even have to do with proof. No, the real reason people reject Christ has to do with their wills. To acknowledge Jesus Christ as Lord would mean:

1. *Having an authority higher than themselves.* It would mean they could no longer run their own lives and live under their own set of rules. They would have to submit their wills to somebody else's; they would have to let God call the shots.

2. *Being humbled.* They would have to admit that all of their education and intellect are of no help. The only way they can get into heaven is by relying on Christ.

3. *Change of lifestyle.* They would have to clean up their acts and obey God.

These are the real reasons people reject Christ. It has nothing to do with proof. It has everything to do with them wanting to be in control. They want to be "The Boss" of their lives.

Ultimate Action

Be transformed by the "Living Spring." Spend some time in prayer, asking Jesus to take total control of your life. Ask Him to clear away the gunk—pride, greed, lust—within you that's holding you back from an abundant life in Him.

ULTIMATE Shepherd!

Week Seven

X

Nothing
can separate
us from
God's love—
not wild
wolves or
natural and
manmade
disasters...
or even
death!

Day 43: Totally Forgiven

"He who is without sin among you, let him throw a stone at her first." And again He stooped down and wrote on the ground. Then those who heard it, being convicted by their conscience, went out one by one, beginning with the oldest even to the last (John 8:7-9 NKJV).

Ultimate Word: *Read John 8:1-11*

Ultimate Encounter

It's morning and Jesus is again teaching at the temple. He's sitting down and the atmosphere is a lot more relaxed—until the Pharisees and the teachers of the law drag in a woman caught in the act of adultery.

Talk about having Jesus cornered! Here He's been doing all of this teaching about God's love and how He wants to give people life. And now suddenly the religious leaders confront Him with somebody that, according to Old Testament law, should actually be executed. What can He do? If He says, "Stone her," all of His talk about love and forgiveness will be a joke. If He says, "Let her go," He'll be saying God's Word is a joke. From every angle it looks like the religious leaders finally have Him trapped.

But Jesus will not be put in a box. They've given Him two choices. So what does He do? He picks a third. (How many times in our own lives have we asked God, "All right, which is it? Choice A or choice B?" Then He comes up with choice W!)

"O.K., you want to kill her?" Jesus says. "Then kill her. But, oh, by the way—make sure that the first one to start the execution isn't guilty of anything himself."

What a phenomenal answer! Once again He's turned a religious, self-righteous group around and forced them to look at their own hearts. And it appears as if they're not too thrilled with what they see.

To this day no one is sure what Jesus wrote when He bent down and scribbled on the ground. Some think it was a list of all the religious leaders' sins. Whatever it was, the accusers began to leave—the oldest first on down to the youngest.

Once again we see the tender, gentle side of Christ's love—the part that wants to forgive sins. It makes no difference what we've done. It doesn't even matter if, as in the woman's case, our sins are worthy of the death penalty. *Jesus wants to forgive us of all that we've ever done wrong.*

Talk about freedom! Imagine knowing that whenever we foul up, whenever we make a mistake, Jesus is there to forgive us. He's always there to pick us up and help us get back on our feet, just as He did with the adulteress. And look how He does it. He doesn't clobber her over the head with guilt. He doesn't go around grandstanding, holding it above her, or trying to make her feel like lizard spit. He gently and tenderly tells her she's forgiven. That's it; end of discussion.

There's one more thing we should keep in mind: Jesus' last words to the woman are "go now and leave your life of sin" (John 8:11).

Ultimate Action

Have you blown it lately? Does your relationship seem a little icy? Confess your sins to Jesus, then accept His forgiveness. He loves you and wants to help you stay on the right track. Anytime you sin, get on your knees and tell God you're sorry. But remember: Your confession can't be fake—you have to truly desire to change and to follow Him.

Day 44: Totally Free

[Jesus] continued, "You are from below; I am from above. You are of this world; I am not of this world. I told you that you would die in your sins; if you do not believe that I am the one I claim to be, you will indeed die in your sins" (John 8:23,24).

Ultimate Word: *Read John 8:12-41*

Ultimate Encounter

Jesus is coming down pretty hard on all the religious bigwigs. Quite a contrast to how kind and gentle He was with the woman who had committed adultery. What's the difference? And how can we make sure He responds to us the way He did to the woman and not the way He did to the Pharisees?

The answer has to do with our hearts. If we're self-righteous and think we have it all together, or if we think we're better than the next person, Jesus' response to us will probably be the same as it was to the religious leaders. If we believe we have it all together, we're lying to ourselves. That would mean we think we really don't need God; we can make it on our own goodness. So Jesus has to shatter our little fantasy worlds and show us what we're really like so we'll turn to Him for help. The woman caught in adultery already knew she needed help. Inside she was already crying out to be saved. And it was that crying out that Jesus responded to.

A short time later, some of the people start to believe in Jesus, so He gives them a little more truth: "Everyone who sins is a slave to sin."

Of course this gets everybody riled but Jesus is delivering a hard-hitting truth. Sin is deceptive. On the outside it usually looks great—lots of fun and grins—a shortcut to good times. But sin is the same today as it was yesterday…a slave maker.

Underneath all the flashy "good-times bait," there lies a hook. We may not feel it at first. In fact, the bait may be so tasty that we just keep on chowing down. But eventually, we bite into the hook. And gradually, without our even knowing it, that hook starts to dig in. Without our knowledge, it starts to control…and there's nothing we can do about it on our own. It makes no difference how smart or careful we are; if we're nibbling on sin, we'll become its slave. It can be anything: sex, drugs, lying, cheating, gossiping, materialism, self-centeredness. You name it, the more we eat the bait, the more it takes control.

But the good news is *Jesus can break that control.* He can free us! Don't ask how; it's pretty hard to figure out. But look around and you'll see it happen hundreds of times in people's lives. Somehow, as we give Him control of our lives and spend time with Him, either the old desires begin to fade or Jesus gives us the power to break them. This doesn't always happen overnight, but if we're really honest in pursuing Him, if we're really honest in wanting to be free of the sin, He'll be there to break its grip and set us free.

Ultimate Action

✔ *Reach for the key to freedom through Christ.* Stand before Him with confession and repentance in your heart. Be ready for His help.

✔ *Accept the power Jesus offers.* Not only does Jesus forgive us when we sin, but He gives us the desire and strength to stop sinning. Praise Him for His grace and mercy.

Day 45: Jesus' Claims

"I am not possessed by a demon," said Jesus, "but I honor my Father and you dishonor me. I am not seeking glory for myself; but there is one who seeks it, and he is the judge. I tell you the truth, if anyone keeps my word, he will never see death" (John 8:49-51).

Ultimate Word: *Read John 8:42-59.*

Ultimate Encounter

Jesus has drawn quite a crowd at the temple courts in Jerusalem, and the Pharisees and hard-hearted Jews are seething at His words. Not only does this unusual guy from Nazareth break the no-work rule by healing people on the Sabbath, but He actually implies that He is God's equal. What's more, He calls God "My Father" instead of "the Father" or "our Father in Heaven."

"He's demon-possessed," the onlookers conclude. "That's the only logical answer. He is a Samaritan, and He is demon-possessed."

The truth is quite the reverse, and Jesus doesn't mince words as He points out their hypocrisy, pride, and greed: "You belong to your father, the devil....My Father, whom you claim as your God, is the one who glorifies me. Though you do not know him, I know him. If I said I did not, I would be a liar like you, but I do know him and keep his word" (John 8:44,54,55).

As if that's not enough to get the crowd's blood boiling, Jesus shares something about His identity that nobody can handle: "I tell you the truth...before Abraham was born, I am!" (verse 58). At that bold claim, many of the people pick up rocks to stone Him, but Jesus hid Himself, slipping away from the temple grounds.

Jesus spoke the truth, yet His words were liked barbed arrows to the unbelieving Jews. Why? Countless people in Jesus' day had reduced their belief in God to a set of external rules; rules they practiced while avoiding any real passion for God or compassion for people. Sound familiar? Just look around and you'll see plenty of phonies dressed up like Christians. But here's a word of caution: If you're gauging Christianity by the actions of others, you'll always be disappointed. Christians are human, which means they're flawed, which means they're prone to mess up.

Now the good news: With the help of the Holy Spirit, all of us can be transformed into the image of the world's only perfect person—Jesus Christ. He's the one we need to focus on. And He's more than a perfect standard...He's a perfect friend.

Ultimate Action

Ask Jesus to peel away the hypocrisy from your own life: "Starting *today*, Jesus, I want to get my eyes off everyone else. I want to put my focus on You. Give me the strength to avoid hypocrisy and to live my faith through my words and actions. Amen."

Day 46: Clear Vision

"While I am in the world, I am the light of the world." When He had said this, He spat on the ground, and made clay of the spittle, and applied the clay to [the blind man's] eyes, and said to him, "Go, wash in the pool of Siloam" (which is translated, Sent). And so he went away and washed, and came back seeing (John 9:5-7 NASB).

Ultimate Word: *Read John 9:1-12*

Ultimate Encounter

Jesus is making a pretty hefty claim: "I am the light of the world." But He has the power to back it up. Any crazy person can claim to be God's gift to the human race—but how many can prove it by giving sight to someone who has *never* seen?

Of course, the method may seem a little weird—a "spit pie" doesn't seem like the best choice in treatment. But keep in mind that customs back then were a little different than today. In the old days, people believed there were medicinal properties in the spit of holy men. Now Jesus probably has a pretty good idea that spit and mud don't give people back their sight. Still, He uses this backward medical practice as something the man can cling to, a security blanket to help the man's frail faith.

But in His love for the man, Jesus does not stop there. He knows that the fellow's faith needs more developing, so He challenges it again, forcing it to grow by sending him across town to wash off the mud. Think about it. Walking through town with a spit-mud pie dripping down your face would be a bit of a stretch for anybody's faith. But the man continued to obey, and his faith continued to grow. And by the end of this little exercise in faith, he could see!

So, what does all this healing have to do with us? We may sometimes feel we lack miserably in the faith department. But the Bible tells us that if we're willing to obey and exercise what little faith we do have, Jesus will work with us. In fact, that's part of who He is…"the author and perfecter of our faith" (Hebrews 12:2).

Ultimate Action

If you are willing to obey and believe as much as you can, Jesus will do the rest.

Day 47: Spiritual Blindness

Jesus said, "For judgment I have come into this world, so that the blind will see and those who see will become blind." Some Pharisees who were with him heard him say this and asked, "What? Are we blind too?" Jesus said, "If you were blind, you would not be guilty of sin; but now that you claim you can see, your guilt remains" (John 9:39-41).

Ultimate Word: *Read John 9:13-41*

Ultimate Encounter

If the phrase "don't confuse me with the facts" ever applied to anyone, it would have to be the Pharisees. Nothing could be plainer; all the witnesses agree. Thanks to Jesus, the man born blind can see. But the Pharisees aren't interested in the facts. Their minds are already made up.

First, the religious leaders interview the man. Then his parents. Then back to the man again. The truth couldn't be clearer. But they keep right on asking until finally it gets to be such a joke that the healed man asks, "How many times do you have to hear this? What's the deal—are you thinking of becoming His disciples, too?"

Of course, they hit the ceiling. They call him a filthy sinner, pat themselves on the back for being so holy, and finally, for good measure, throw him out of the synagogue and out of their religion.

Poor guy. First, he staggers around town with a mud compress, then he receives sight for the very first time, then he's interrogated by the Pharisees, and finally, to top it off, he's excommunicated. (In his culture, this not only isolates him from his faith, family, and friends, but also makes finding any type of work close to impossible.)

Talk about having "one of those days." But it should be a real encouragement for us to see that Jesus doesn't desert the man. He makes a point of searching him out again and continues to help.

And the man's response? Here was a guy who started out needing so much help in the faith department that Jesus used a questionable medical practice to enable him to exercise his faith. By the end of the day this same man is not only seeing and believing in Jesus, but, according to verse 38, he's one of the first ever to worship Him!

The healed man shows pretty impressive growth spiritually. And all because Jesus stayed with him throughout the process—just as He does with us, regardless of what we're going through and regardless of how long it takes. God is never done working with us. Even when we think He's done enough, He's always there with us, always ready to keep on helping, encouraging, and reaching out.

The bottom line? *Jesus will always be next to us, helping us to see and grow.*

Ultimate Action

Consider this fact: Just as Jesus' love and truth opened the blind man's eyes, it has closed and blinded those who pride themselves on "seeing." What does this mean? What is your area of blindness? What would you like to see better?

Day 48: The Good Shepherd

I am the good shepherd; I know my sheep and
my sheep know me—just as the Father knows
me and I know the Father—and I lay down my
life for the sheep (John 10:14,15).

Ultimate Word: *Read John 10:1-21*

Ultimate Encounter

There is no better picture of Jesus' deep love and total
commitment to us than His example of being our Shepherd. To get the full scope of what He's talking about, keep
in mind that the life of a dedicated shepherd meant total
devotion to the flock—a devotion that included putting the
sheep's lives above his own.

First of all, there were thieves and robbers. These dis-
honest men would try to lure away and steal stray lambs.
They weren't interested in the animals' welfare; they were
only interested in the money they could get from them.

Sound familiar? Unfortunately there's more than a few
of those folks around today—people who have turned
Christianity into the business of bucks instead of the commitment of love. But Jesus makes it clear that *if we honestly
seek God*, we'll eventually be able to tell His voice from the
crooks'.

Second, there were plenty of wild animals back then—
mostly wolves. Whenever they closed in, fierce and rav-
enous from hunger, the hired hands usually split. Why
should they risk their lives for somebody else's property?

But the committed shepherd never looked upon his flock as property. He had grown to know and love each of them as individuals. In fact, his love and dedication to them was so intense that he would fight to the death to protect them.

Then there was the hazardous terrain on which the sheep grazed, a dangerous landscape of holes, cliffs, and ravines. Knowing these pitfalls, the caring shepherd would never push or drive his flock. Instead, he would walk ahead of them, carefully scouting out the safest routes and gently leading them into areas he had already checked out.

Good pasture was also important. Grazing was about the only thing the sheep did, so why not make it as pleasant for them as possible? A sensitive shepherd would go to great risks to find the best grazing land for his sheep to make their lives as happy and healthy as possible.

And finally, there were the hillside pens, places where the animals could gather for protection during the night. To make sure the sheep were really safe, the shepherd would sleep on the ground at the entrance of the pen. He would literally act as a human gate, a gate that would serve as the only means to reach the flock.

By comparing Himself to a shepherd, this is the tender, intense, all-giving love Jesus promises:

✔ He will protect us from evil.

✔ He will fight off any enemy that's trying to destroy us.

✔ He will go before us in every situation.

✔ He will give us a happy and full life.

Be confident of this truth: Jesus will lay down His own life for us. In fact, He already did—on the cross.

Ultimate Action

There's a war going on—an ancient spiritual struggle that's as real as any physical conflict that takes place on this planet. And as you see in today's lesson, the Good Shepherd is your protector. But you have some important responsibilities in this conflict of the cosmos. Go down the following checklist and make sure you're doing your part to stay under God's protection:

✔ View church and Bible studies as training time.

✔ Obey Christ. Don't make choices based on what is easiest, but on the basis of what God says is best.

✔ Through consistent Bible reading and prayer, learn to hear His voice through all the conflicting messages that bombard you every day.

✔ When an activity starts to take your attention away from Jesus, reevaluate your priorities.

Day 49: Stubborn Skeptics

Why then do you accuse me of blasphemy because I said, "I am God's Son"? Do not believe me unless I do what my Father does. But if I do it, even though you do not believe me, believe the miracles, that you may know and understand that the Father is in me, and I in the Father (John 10:36-38).

Ultimate Word: *Read John 10:22-42*

Ultimate Encounter

Can you believe Jesus' phenomenal patience? Here He is, healing people, performing miracles, and making it super clear to the folks that He is God, the Son. So what does everybody ask? "How long are You going to keep us in suspense—tell us who You are." Come on, people!

Once again Jesus has to teach the people that it really doesn't matter if they have all the facts. The only people who are going to believe are the ones that really want to follow God. Following God is a matter of obedience, not human logic.

To prove His point, Jesus goes ahead and tells them not once, but twice, who He is. And, sure enough, instead of dropping to their knees and crying, "We understand, forgive us," they try to kill Him—not once, but twice: "Again the Jews picked up the stones" (verse 31) and "again they tried to seize him" (verse 39).

Sadly, many people today aren't interested in knowing God either. Despite what they say, most really aren't looking for proof. If they were really sincere, they could seek God, as Jesus suggested, and find the truth. The facts are available for anyone who's really interested. It isn't a lack of facts that prevents people from receiving Jesus Christ. Today, just as it was back then, the problem is with the human will.

Ultimate Action

Hundreds of books exist that scientifically, historically, archeologically, even mathematically, show that Christ has to be who He says He is. In fact, some people, including Josh McDowell, have set out to disprove Christ but, by the end of their research, have become true believers in Him. One book you just have to get your hands on is a classic, must-have resource: *Evidence That Demands a Verdict,* by Josh McDowell (Campus Crusade for Christ). This is an interesting yet thorough book that has captivated young people with the facts demonstrating the truth of the Bible and Jesus Christ.

ULTIMATE Love!

Week Eight

X

Jesus'
love
revealed—
in the
form of
passionate,
hope-filled
messages,
healing,
and lots of
patience.

Day 50: Love Is Patient

A man named Lazarus was sick....When he heard this, Jesus said, "This sickness will not end in death. No, it is for God's glory so that God's Son may be glorified through it." Jesus loved Martha and her sister and Lazarus. Yet when he heard that Lazarus was sick, he stayed where he was two more days (John 11:1,4-6).

Ultimate Word: *Read John 11:1-16*

Ultimate Encounter

Lazarus and Jesus were the best of buddies. And since Jesus was always showing His love for others, and since the two were such good friends, Martha and Mary naturally figured Jesus would race to their brother's aid.

Not quite. Instead, Jesus waits a few more days until Lazarus is good and dead. Why? What gives?

God wants to bless us, usually more than we can imagine. But often, especially when we're young, our timetables are radically different from His. We're out there wanting to rush it, to Grand Prix it—to get everything now while the getting's good. Meanwhile, God's out there saying, "Hold on a minute. If you just wait another second and leave it to Me, I'll make it even better." Unfortunately, by not waiting we usually wind up with our second-rate desire instead of God's first-rate plan. Instead of waiting on His time schedule so the fruit can ripen and sweeten, our fears and impatience tell us to grab it now when it's still green and bitter.

We keep forgetting that God sees the whole picture; He knows the precise day of picking. He knows when that fruit we want so desperately will be at its peak. If we let Him, He'll always wait until the perfect moment before harvesting that fruit and answering our prayers. Not a minute too early; not a minute too late.

By abiding by Jesus' timetable, Mary, Martha, and Lazarus' lives are going to be much more fruitful and exciting than if they could have forced God to follow their own schedule.

Ultimate Action

During those times when it seems as if God has completely missed the boat—when your hopes and dreams seem totally dead—hold tight and trust Jesus. If you wait on Him, you'll wind up with greater life than you could possibly have expected. Waiting isn't always the easiest, but if it's what God wants, it will always be the best.

Memorize this verse:

But those who wait on the LORD shall renew their strength; they shall mount up with wings like eagles, they shall run and not be weary, they shall walk and not faint (Isaiah 40:31 NKJV).

Day 51: God Cries

When Jesus saw her weeping, and the Jews who had come along with her also weeping, he was deeply moved in spirit and troubled. "Where have you laid him?" he asked.

"Come and see, Lord," they replied.

Jesus wept (John 11:33-35).

Ultimate Word: *Read John 11:17-37*

Ultimate Encounter

Lazarus is dead, and Jesus has gone to his tomb. Lazarus' sisters, Martha and Mary, were disappointed that Jesus hadn't rushed there to heal their brother before he died. They said, "Lord if you had been here, my brother would not have died."

Jesus was deeply moved by the sorrow He saw all around Him. And "Jesus wept."

Now He makes a startling claim: "I am the resurrection and the life. He who believes in me will live, even though he dies; and whoever lives and believes in me will never die" (John 11:25,26).

Notice, He doesn't say, "I'll show you the way to live so you won't die." Instead, He says *He* is the life, *He* is the resurrection! Jesus is not offering a new set of rules that we have to follow. He is offering a relationship, a relationship with Himself. He is the "bread of life." He is the "living water." He is the "resurrection and the life."

Jesus wept. Ever since we were little tykes in Sunday school, we've been taught that this is the shortest verse in the Bible. But God has more in mind than impressing us with His sentence construction. Instead, this verse and those surrounding it give us an even clearer picture of Jesus' personality.

In this passage, we see that Jesus is "deeply moved" with grief not once, not twice, but three times! (See John 11:33,35,38.) Why? Doesn't He think He'll see Lazarus again? Doesn't He think He can pull off this raising-of-the-dead bit? Of course He does. It's pretty obvious that Jesus knows exactly what He can do.

Have you noticed that every time Jesus is overcome with sadness in this passage it's because the people around Him are overcome with mourning? Could it be any clearer how deeply God loves us, how strongly He feels for us? It makes no difference that He knows the final outcome will be good; if we're hurting, God's hurting.

Our Lord is not a whip-snapping ringmaster who expects us to jump through hoops every time He shouts. He's not a sadistic tyrant just waiting to push us into hell over the slightest mistake. He doesn't say, "I'm sorry, Billy, you're just two points shy of heaven. It's the burning pit for you, Bub."

That's not our God.

Instead, He is constantly at our sides, loving us and encouraging us. He is always there, feeling what we're feeling. He's excited over our victories and aches over our defeats. And, just as with Mary and Martha, every time we weep, He weeps.

That's commitment.
That's caring.
That's love.

Ultimate Action

Stop knocking yourself out trying to earn your salvation by being extra good or extra religious. That's as impossible as a baseball glove trying to play center field on its own. It can flap around out there all it wants, but it's not likely it will make any great plays. It isn't until the glove is filled by its owner's hand that it really comes to life.

The same is true with you. The abundant life Jesus keeps promising depends on how much you let the owner—Jesus—have His way. To what extent will you allow Him to fill you? Talk to Jesus about it today.

Day 52: Arise!

He cried with a loud voice, "Lazarus, come forth!" And he who had died came out bound hand and foot with graveclothes, and his face was wrapped with a cloth. Jesus said to them, "Loose him, and let him go" (John 11:43,44 NKJV).

Ultimate Word: *Read John 11:38-44*

Ultimate Encounter

"Lazarus, come forth!" And Lazarus did! Another example of Jesus' power over life and death. Raising someone from the dead wasn't a one time thing for Jesus. As we've already mentioned, in His three short years of ministry Jesus brought at least four different people back from the dead.

There was Lazarus, of course. And there was Jairus' 12-year-old daughter whose death devastated him and his wife (Luke 8:41-56). There was the time Jesus actually stopped a funeral heading for the cemetery and raised a young man out of the coffin (Luke 7:11-16). And finally, of course, there was Jesus' own resurrection.

Four for four. Not a bad record.

Besides showing Jesus' power and proving He is who He says He is, how does raising people from the dead apply to the living? The problem with death is it comes in many forms. We don't have to be lying in some grave to experience it. We may be young and alive on the outside, but inside there may be parts of us that have already died—dreams shattered, hopes destroyed, pieces of our lives broken and withered. For most of us, those areas may seem just as impossible to resurrect and bring back to life as raising some smelly, four-day-old corpse.

But, as we've seen, there is a way for resurrection. And it always starts and finishes with Jesus. Still, there are a couple of requirements on our part. First, we have to...

Believe

Let's get back to Lazarus' life story: What does Jesus tell Martha? "Did I not tell you that if you believed, you would see the glory of God?" (John 11:40). Then there are His other promises: "If you believe, you will receive whatever you ask for in prayer" (Matthew 21:22). "Everything is possible for him who believes" (Mark 9:23).

But belief isn't something we can use to manipulate God. He isn't a vending machine that we drop belief coins into and out pops the answers to our every whim. That would be only *partial* belief. *Full* belief involves trusting God more deeply. It involves trusting that if we ask for the wrong thing, God loves us enough to step in and give us what we really need.

A child who has no understanding of nutrition may want to chow down on candy bars. He may cry and kick and scream when he doesn't get his way. In fact, he'll probably accuse his parents of hating him when they not only say no but also make him eat his vegetables. But we have to admit that we would question the love of any parent who constantly gives in to candy bar demands. It's the same way with God. What kind of love would He have for us if He always gave us what we *think* we need, instead of what He *knows* we need?

The first step to trusting Jesus is belief—believing that God can and will answer each of our prayers. It also means believing that He may give us something far better than what we're asking for.

However, believing is only half of the solution to resurrection. The other half is to ...

Obey

If Martha and Mary had not obeyed and had refused to roll the boulder away, it would have been a little tough for Lazarus to come out of the tomb. Obedience isn't always easy. The sisters are in a tough spot. Would you want to open up somebody's grave after he'd been rotting inside for four days? Talk about bad B.O.! And what about their embarrassment if it didn't work out. But they don't seem to hesitate. Once they fully understand the Lord's command, they're willing to obey even if it means looking like idiots.

How obedient are we? Are we doing all that God asks of us? Or are there certain areas of our lives that we're still holding out on because we don't really trust Him or we are afraid we'll look like idiots? We need to fully believe in Christ in all things!

Ultimate Action

✔ *Let go; trust God.* If you give up those strong-holds of independence and let Him have control of them, you will be amazed at how He brings you to a better life than you thought possible.

✔ *Be willing to believe and obey.* If you are, the very thing you think is dead—the good that is rotting and seemingly impossible to save—will be given new and abundant life.

Day 53: The Plot Sickens

Now the chief priests and the Pharisees had given orders that if anyone knew where He was, he should report it, that they might seize Him (John 11:57 NASB).

Ultimate Word: *Read John 11:45-57*

Ultimate Encounter

Throughout Jesus' ministry the Pharisees kept asking for a sign, for proof of Jesus' claim to be the Messiah. (See Matthew 12:38; 16:1.)

Well, they definitely had a sign now. Jesus raised Lazarus from the dead. And signs don't come much fancier than a man raised from the grave after being dead four days. What did the Pharisees do after this miraculous sign? "So from that day on they [the priests and Pharisees] plotted to take [Jesus'] life" (John 11:53).

But what's even more interesting is that these guys don't doubt that the miracles are really happening. In fact, they are the ones saying, "Here is this man performing many miraculous signs" (John 11:47).

As we've noted before, proof and facts are not what prevent people from believing in Christ. Just as with the

Pharisees, it comes down to us giving up control and ownership of our lives.

Granted, personal control can be a pretty scary thing to lose. But looking at Jesus' track record with all His power, all His love, and all His authority over death, and then looking at our own track record, well, we don't have to be rocket scientists to figure out who we should let call the shots.

But even with all His power, Jesus still uses some common sense. Instead of hanging out in an area where people are trying to kill Him (Lazarus lived just a short stroll from Jerusalem), Jesus and the guys opt for a little R&R in the desert.

There's a lesson here for us. Yes, we should have faith; yes, we should trust God in every situation. But He also expects us to use our brains.

Ultimate Action

Understand that the question, "Why bother studying for the chemistry test when I already prayed?" isn't exactly the type of faith God has in mind. Faith is not an excuse for laziness or stupidity. It is a way for God to be glorified and for you to reach your fullest, ultimate life.

Day 54: Royal Welcome

As they approached Jerusalem...Jesus sent two of his disciples, saying to them, "Go to the village ahead of you, and just as you enter it, you will find a colt tied there, which no one has ever ridden...." When they brought the colt to Jesus and threw their cloaks over it, he sat on it (Mark 11:1,2,7).

Ultimate Word: *Read Mark 11:1-11*

Ultimate Encounter

As Jesus approaches Jerusalem, He tells His disciples to fetch an unridden donkey colt. (An unridden colt was often kept in a village for important visitors.) Jesus' disciples know at once what He is saying by mounting this colt: He is claiming to be the fulfillment of Zechariah 9:9:

> Rejoice greatly, O Daughter of Zion! Shout, Daughter of Jerusalem! See, your king comes to you, righteous and having salvation, gentle and riding on a donkey, on a colt, the foal of a donkey.

Jesus is announcing that He is coming to the capital as its king.

The disciples envision the action: Jesus will ride in past cheering crowds, ascend the temple steps, march into the inner court, and grasp the horns at the corners of the altar. This will signify that He is declaring His kingship. All the people will rise against the Romans, and with the power of God behind them, the Jews will quickly oust the pagans and institute the kingdom of God.

Guess again, guys.

The crowds do cheer. They even fill the road with cloaks and tree branches to create a royal carpet. Christ *was* entering Jerusalem as King, but not quite the kind the Jews imagined. As they would soon discover, He wasn't coming as a political leader; He was coming as the *spiritual king*.

The next time Jesus comes, He'll come as king of the physical world. But this first time He came to conquer Satan and become ruler of our hearts, minds, and souls—and to give us ultimate love.

Ultimate Action

As a Christian you need to recognize that Satan is your enemy, but he's an enemy Christ defeated on the cross. Even though we have victory in Jesus, the battle here on earth isn't over yet. Even though you're a child of the King, Satan will do anything he can to trip you up.

But you have power through Jesus. You can stand strong against the devil and never cower or panic. Memorize this verse and hold on to its truth the next time you feel the heat of spiritual warfare: "You, dear children, are from God and have overcome them, because the one who is in you is greater than the one who is in the world" (1 John 4:4).

Day 55: Radical Worship

Then Mary took about a pint of pure nard, an expensive perfume; she poured it on Jesus' feet and wiped his feet with her hair (John 12:3).

Ultimate Word: *Read John 12:1-7*

Ultimate Encounter

After some time in the desert, Jesus and His disciples return to Lazarus' home. Mary, in her deep love and appreciation for Jesus, pours expensive perfume all over His feet and then, to top it off, begins wiping His feet with her hair! Talk about love. Talk about devotion. Talk about strange!

Think about it: Somebody kneels down and begins washing your feet, a common custom back then. But the person uses her hair to wipe your feet! It would probably make you a tad uncomfortable. But not Jesus. He accepts it. He doesn't ridicule the woman for her style; He doesn't tell her she's out of line. Instead, He recognizes that what she's doing is from her heart—and it's the heart that God looks at.

Extravagant? Lavish? Impulsive? Generous? Absolutely!

"But one of his disciples, Judas Iscariot...objected. Why wasn't this perfume sold and the money given to the poor?" But Judas isn't interested in the poor. His focus is the jingle in the old money bag, which could have been a lot louder if Mary would have come across with some cold, hard cash instead of spending it on perfume.

The point is that we can't buy off God. If it comes down to one or the other, He'd much rather have our hearts than our money. As we give our hearts to Christ, He will pour Himself into us many times over.

Ultimate Action

Don't let your faith become mechanical, full of heartless ritual and meaningless tradition.

Spend some time alone, quietly worshiping Jesus and telling Him how much you love Him. Ask Him to be with you: "Lord, help me to love You with a pure heart...one without hidden motives. Fill me with the fullness of Your love."

Day 56: Total Surrender

Jesus replied, "The hour has come for the Son of Man to be glorified. I tell you the truth, unless a kernel of wheat falls to the ground and dies, it remains only a single seed. But if it dies, it produces many seeds" (John 12:23,24).

Ultimate Word: *Read John 12:20-36*

Ultimate Encounter

There's a lot happening in today's Scripture passage. Jesus' teachings and miracles are awesome, but they're just frosting on the cake. What's the main reason for Jesus' leaving the good times in heaven and slumming it down here on earth? He explains that He's going to die: "the hour has come." In fact He makes it painfully clear how important this dying business is: "It was for this very reason I came" (John 12:27). Then Jesus says: "Father, glorify your name!"

After Jesus speaks, the crowd suddenly hears from heaven the voice of God the Father praising His Son. Not your everyday occurrence, and most people are pretty impressed. But of course there's always somebody trying to give God's miracle a "natural" explanation. "Must've been thunder. Yeah, yeah, that's it. It was, uh, thunder." Of course, hearing thunder boom out a complete sentence would, in itself, be quite a miracle: "I have glorified it, and will glorify it again." (For the record, this is the third time people have heard God talk to His Son. The other times were when Jesus was baptized [Luke 3:22] and when three dead-and-gone Old Testament heroes appeared beside Him on a mountaintop [Luke 9:35].)

An important section in today's reading is where Jesus says, "Unless a kernel of wheat falls to the ground and dies, it remains only a single seed. But if it dies, it produces many seeds. The man who loves his life will lose it, while the man who hates his life in this world will keep it for eternal life" (John 12:24,25).

Once more Jesus is making it clear that if you want to live, you have to die—you have to give up, you have to stop trying to run your own life. You have to turn it over to God. By life, He's not just talking about these living, breathing carcasses we're tooling around in. He's talking about our every hope, our every dream, our loves, our hates—everything that we are, everything that makes us up.

A tall order? Absolutely. But there's a cool principle here that's just as absolute as gravity or any other law in the universe. Somehow, when we let ourselves die and give God all that we are, He turns around and fills us with Himself, making us a hundred times better.

Ultimate Action

✔ *You can't outgive God.* Giving is tough—there's no doubt about it. Death, no matter how you look at it, is no picnic. But here's the good news: When a grain of wheat falls and dies in the ground it eventually sprouts and bears more grain, which sprout and bear even more—until the initial death has led to life a thousand times over.

✔ *Surrender everything to Christ.* When we give God our talents, our hopes, our lives—when we die to them (either emotionally or literally)—they return in greater portion and abundance than we can possibly imagine. That's Jesus' promise, and it always happens. *Always!*

ULTIMATE Readiness!

Week Nine

Uncovering
vital
insights
about
always
being
ready.

Day 57: A Trick Question

As [Jesus] taught the people in the temple and preached the gospel...the chief priests and the scribes, together with the elders, confronted Him and spoke to Him, saying, "Tell us, by what authority are You doing these things?..." But He answered and said to them, "I also will ask you one thing, and answer Me: The baptism of John— was it from heaven or from men?" (Luke 20:1-4 NKJV).

Ultimate Word: *Read Luke 20:1-18*

Ultimate Encounter

Jesus continues to teach in the temple (built to worship God, but now the stronghold of the people who are trying to kill His Son). The chief priests, scribes, and elders demand to know who gave Jesus the authority to teach, heal, and act so boldly. They're not nearly as concerned with the truth as they are about trying to trip up Jesus. If Jesus slips just once, they can arrest Him for breaking either Jewish law or Roman law.

Knowing they are already aware of His claims as Messiah, Jesus throws the question back to them. "Tell me, John's baptism—was it from heaven or from men?" What a dilemma. If they admit that the baptism was from God, then they have to accept John's claims that Jesus is the Messiah. Even though John has baptized thousands of Jews, the religious leaders pretend they don't know. Jesus, knowing they know, refuses to tell them where His authority comes from. Instead, he begins a parable:

> A man planted a vineyard, rented it to some farmers and went away for a long time. At harvest time he sent a servant to the tenants so they would give him some of the fruit of the vineyard. But the tenants beat him and sent him away empty-handed. He sent another servant, but that one also they beat and treated shamefully and sent away empty-handed. He sent still a third, and they wounded him and threw him out.
>
> But when the tenants saw him, they talked the matter over. "This is the heir," they said. "Let's kill him, and the inheritance will be ours." So they threw him out of the vineyard and killed him.
>
> What then will the owner of the vineyard do to them? He will come and kill those tenants and give the vineyard to others (Luke 20:9-12,14-16).

What is Jesus really telling the religious leaders?

God has planted a vineyard (Israel) and put His chosen people (the Jews) in charge of it. Through the years, He has sent several prophets to the people, asking them to receive His message concerning His proper place in their lives. But they refuse to believe the prophets and beat them. Still, God in His patience continues sending more prophets, and still the people refuse to listen to them. Finally, He sends His Son, but the people kill Him. As a result, God promises to destroy the unfaithful vine growers and give the vineyard to others.

Ultimate Action

✔ *Is Jesus the most important person in your life?* If not, take the steps to put Him first. Ask Jesus to help you put Him first. Reading the Bible and attending church and Sunday school will also help you focus on Jesus.

✔ *Are you confident that you'll spend eternity with Christ?* What gives you this confidence? How can you communicate this to others?

Day 58: An Absurd Question

"Teacher," they said, "Moses wrote for us that if a man's brother dies and leaves a wife but no children, the man must marry the widow and have children for his brother. Now there were seven brothers. The first one married a woman and died childless. The second and then the third married her, and in the same way the seven died, leaving no children. Finally, the woman died too. Now then, at the resurrection whose wife will she be, since the seven were married to her?" (Luke 20:28-33).

Ultimate Word: *Read Luke 20:27-47*

Ultimate Encounter

The Sadducees, who do not believe in the resurrection (life after death), try to make Jesus look ridiculous and prove Him wrong with the absurd question quoted above. Jesus points out that their entire argument is based on a wrong assumption: that life carries on in heaven as it does on earth. Jesus continues to point out that life after death is a fact, not something to waste time arguing about. When describing Himself to Moses, God explained that He is still the God of Abraham, Isaac, and Jacob—meaning that they are still living (Leviticus 26:42). We see that Jesus' answer is so impressive that no one has the courage to question Him any longer about anything. In fact, some of the teachers respond, "Well said, teacher!"

But the people have many more wrong ideas, and Jesus tries to correct them. He asks, "How is it that they say the Christ is the Son of David?" They know from prophecies that the Messiah will be a descendant of David, and they are correct. Jesus is making the point that He is not only from the line of David, but He is also David's Lord. "The Lord said to my lord," David wrote in the book of Psalms. Once again Jesus makes it clear that He's God.

Finally, Jesus warns the people about the scribes, men who say they love God but who are much more concerned about building their own kingdoms than working to build God's.

Beware of the teachers of the law. They like to walk around in flowing robes and love to be greeted in the marketplaces and have the most important seats in the synagogues and the places of honor at banquets. They devour widows' houses and for a show make lengthy prayers. Such men will be punished most severely (Luke 20:46,47).

Although Jesus gave this warning almost 2,000 years ago, it still is true today. There are "leaders" and people in today's Christian circles that are in it more for the show and the bucks than for the Lord.

How can we know who to listen to? Check out the fruit they're bearing and compare their teachings to what Jesus says.

Ultimate Action

✔ *Thank Jesus for the gift of life.* When you pray, thank God for creating you in His image and for giving you a reason for existence. Discover how important you are to God by reading Psalm 139. Copy this psalm on a sheet of paper and tape it above your bed.

✔ *Pray for discernment.* Ask God to help you know His truth. Also pray for church leaders and other people who represent Christianity. Pray that they, too, will have Christ-centered discernment.

Day 59: Wired to Win

For I will give you words and wisdom that none of your adversaries will be able to resist or contradict. You will be betrayed even by parents, brothers, relatives and friends, and they will put some of you to death. All men will hate you because of me. But not a hair of your head will perish. By standing firm you will gain life (Luke 21:15-19).

Ultimate Word: *Read Luke 21*

Ultimate Encounter

In today's Ultimate Word passage, the rich noisily drop their large offerings into the collection box while a poor widow puts in all she has, two lepta (a small copper coin worth about one-eighth of a cent). Jesus notices and points out that she has contributed more than all of the other people combined. Why? She's given all that she has, not because she feels an obligation, but because she trusts that the Lord will provide for her needs.

Then some of Jesus' disciples point out the splendor of the temple, and Jesus prophesies that everything they see will be torn down. Everything. The temple is used to worship God, but if the people refuse God what good is it? It becomes nothing but a worthless shell, another empty ritual in the name of "religion."

The men ask for signs as to when this destruction will take place. Instead of a definite date, Jesus gives them events that will lead up to it. Carefully read Jesus' descriptions. Although He's referring to the destruction of Jerusalem in A.D. 70, keep in mind that many of the same events will also happen before His second coming (see the book of Revelation).

Jesus warns, "Watch out that you are not deceived. For many will come in my name, claiming, 'I am he,' and 'The time is near.' Do not follow them." Many people will say they are Christians or even that they are the Messiah, but they're deceivers. Jesus goes on to say that there will be many wars, famines, plagues, even signs from heaven; but that we are not to worry. God is in control, and He will protect the faithful.

Recent studies indicate that more than 60 percent of the world is under some sort of religious persecution or is about to fall under that persecution. Today, in some communist and Muslim countries, Christians are still undergoing torture, beatings, and even death for practicing their beliefs. According to Jesus, these things will only increase. But we don't have to be scared. Scripture assures us that we shouldn't be afraid—just faithful. We will even have many opportunities to share Jesus with an unsaved world, plus Christ will give us the words to reach their hearts.

Ultimate Action

Study the following verse:

Not that I have already obtained all this, or have already been made perfect, but I press on to take hold of that for which Christ Jesus took hold of me. Brothers, I do not consider myself yet to have taken hold of it. But one thing I do: Forgetting what is behind and straining toward what is ahead, I press on toward the goal to win the prize for which God has called me heavenward in Christ Jesus (Philippians 3:12-14).

✔ How is the Christian life like a big race?

✔ Think of some things in life that cause you to stumble and veer off the path God has set before you.

✔ What are some things you need to do in order to stay spiritually strong, especially when "world pressures" heat up?

Day 60: Lord of the Towel

So when He had washed their feet, taken His garments, and sat down again, He said to them, "Do you know what I have done to you? You call Me Teacher and Lord, and you say well, for so I am. If I then, your Lord and Teacher, have washed your feet, you also ought to wash one another's feet. For I have given you an example, that you should do as I have done to you" (John 13:12-15 NKJV).

Ultimate Word: *Read John 13:1-17*

Ultimate Encounter

Jesus has fewer than 24 hours left on earth when this Passover passage takes place. He has a lot of last-minute things to say, and John doesn't miss a word. In fact, nearly a third of the Gospel of John is spent on these last few hours—hours that, more clearly than any others in history, reveal the true personality of God. Let's look at some of the highlights:

Passover Symbolism

Here it is, the Passover supper, the once-a-year meal celebrating how God freed the Jews from Egypt. But Jesus turns everything around and suddenly gives the meal a completely different meaning. In fact, in the other three Gospels (Matthew, Mark, and Luke) we see Him take portions of the supper, the bread and wine, and explain how they no longer represent the people's freedom from Egypt. Instead, they now represent Him—His sacrificed body and shed blood that will free people from even tougher enslavement, the enslavement to sin and its punishment.

The Depth of God's Love

Custom at this time calls for the host's servant to wash the guests' feet. But since there is no host where Jesus and His friends are eating, there is no servant. Other Gospel accounts talk about how the disciples have been arguing over which of them is the greatest, so there's a good chance most of them are pretty worried about who's going to get the bottom-of-the-barrel job of feet washing.

So what does Jesus do? He strips down to what would be His underwear and begins washing each of the disciples' feet. Picture that for a moment. God, the Creator of the entire universe, kneeling in His underwear, washing the smelly feet of men! What a perfect picture. What a perfect example of God's heart, of the depth of His love and commitment to each of us. And what a perfect example to demonstrate what God considers to be real greatness.

How to Be Great

Who is great? It's not the world leaders, the Wall Street wizards, the Hollywood superstars, or the Super Bowl champs. It's not even the great spiritual leaders of our times. These people aren't always who God considers great. According to the Lord, it's often just the opposite. According to God, "Whoever wants to become great among you must be your servant, and whoever wants to be first must be your slave—just as the Son of Man did not come to be served, but to serve" (Matthew 20:26-28).

This is real greatness. This is why the Father honors His Son so much. And this is the greatness that the Son wants us to experience.

Ultimate Action

Ask Jesus to continually show you what real greatness is and to give you opportunities to experience and exercise that greatness.

Examine your heart. Are you willing to be a servant? Are you willing to put other people before you? Ask God to give you a servant's heart and a willingness to do as God commands.

Day 61: Ultimate Friendship

A new commandment I give to you, that you love one another, even as I have loved you, that you also love one another. By this all men will know that you are My disciples, if you have love for one another (John 13:34,35 NASB).

Ultimate Word: *Read John 13:18-38*

Ultimate Encounter

After washing the feet of His disciples and instructing them in serving, Jesus reveals that He will be betrayed. He is deeply troubled. Once again we see Him having a tough time of it emotionally. One of the twelve, a friend who has been at His side for three years, who has witnessed and experienced the miracles, who has heard the teachings, who has seen the power—one of the men whose feet Jesus has just washed—is about to turn on Him.

Do you know what's really interesting? We don't see anger, we don't hear harsh words. All we see is Jesus aching over the loss of one of His friends. At last Jesus overcomes the pain and is able to continue. He has so much to say and so little time. Again He explains that He is about to leave. But before He goes, He gives His disciples—and us—a new commandment—a commandment to love one another. Not with the gushy, on-again off-again, heart-flutter stuff we call love, but to love with a dedication and commitment so intense for their fellow brothers and sisters in Christ that regardless of whether it made them feel good or not they would lay down their lives for others. Now that's love!

The same is true today. Jesus isn't looking to punish those who have walked away from Him to follow the world. But He knows that if they don't return they'll eventually be judged. And for that reason, He aches. He weeps. And He waits.

The same goes with His command for us to love other Christians. It's not an option; it's a command. Pretty sobering, especially with all the fighting and competition between various people, churches, and denominations these days. It's hard enough to get some of us to even work together, let alone be willing to lay down our lives for one another. But that's what He commands.

Ultimate Action

Jesus doesn't say you have to agree with every doctrine, belief, or practice that another Christian holds to. You can disagree and debate all you want. The key is to not let diversity turn into division.

Check your heart. Is there any part of you that is prejudiced or bigoted against another sincere, Scripture-based Christian? If so, ask God to help you get rid of it.

Day 62 : Prince of Peace

I am the way and the truth and the life. No one comes to the Father except through me. If you really knew me, you would know my Father as well. From now on, you do know him and have seen him (John 14:6,7).

Ultimate Word: *Read John 14:1-14*

Ultimate Encounter

After explaining to His disciples that He is going away, Jesus tells them to keep trusting. He says, "Do not let your hearts be troubled." In essence He's saying, "Things are going to get pretty hairy for a while, but you've got to hang on. You won't understand all that's about to happen, but I've taken you this far, so believe I won't let you down now."

Thomas still hasn't figured it all out. Jesus says He's going some place and Tom wants to know how to get there. The Lord explains that the only way to get where He's going is through Him. There is only one road to heaven, one way of reaching God. It's not through some philosophy or by being ultrareligious. There is one way and one way only—through Jesus Christ: "I am the way and the truth and the life. *No one* comes to the Father except *through Me.*"

Talk about being straightforward. If it were anybody but Jesus you'd think this guy has an ego problem. When Philip asks Jesus to "show us the Father and that will be enough for us," Jesus' answer is even more to the point: "Anyone who has seen me has seen the Father." Whew! But Jesus can't candy-coat the facts any longer. Time is running out, and His disciples had better get it all straight now because there'll be no second chance.

But sensing that His claims may still be a little too radical for them to handle, Jesus appeals to His past track record: "Come on, guys, if you still don't believe Me, then take a look at what I've done—the miracles, the voice from heaven, the raising of the dead. What more can I do to convince you?" And He points out that they ain't seen nothin' yet! If they keep believing in Him, they'll be doing even *greater* works.

Well, if the fellows weren't hyperventilating before, they're definitely sucking air now. It's one thing for this miracle-worker to claim to be God, but to have Him start saying that they'll be doing the same miracles—and even greater things!—wow!

But it's true. Later, in the book of Acts, we read about the disciples performing miracles. And what's even more interesting is that miracles are still happening today. If you visit the remote regions of Asia, you'll meet Christians who have been imprisoned and beaten for their faith. You'll meet Christians whose lives have been threatened more times than they can count. And you'll meet Christians who have healed the blind and deaf, cast out demons, and raised people from the dead.

Jesus promised it then, and it's still happening today. Jesus said, "I will do whatever you ask in my name, so that the Son may bring glory to the Father. You may ask me for anything in my name, and I will do it" (John 14:13,14).

Ultimate Action

Jesus has laid out a pretty hefty down payment for us—His life. And even though you may not understand the tough times when they come, Jesus has invested too much to just forget about us. He's standing with you now if you've asked Him to. And He'll never leave. Never! Need help? Turn to Jesus.

Day 63: One with God

I will not leave you as orphans; I will come to you. Before long, the world will not see me anymore, but you will see me. Because I live, you also will live. On that day you will realize that I am in my Father, and you are in me, and I am in you (John 14:18-20).

Ultimate Word: *Read John 14:15-31*

Ultimate Encounter

Three times Jesus says that if we love Him we will follow His commandments. It's important to keep that order in mind. First, we are to love Jesus. Then, because of that love, we obey Him. So, first we establish a relationship with Him and, as a result of that love, we start doing what He asks. Our obedience acts as a spiritual thermometer to let us know if we really love Jesus or if we're just playing church.

Two times in our Ultimate Word passage, Jesus talks about sending the Comforter, the Holy Spirit. No doubt the disciples are pretty bummed that Jesus is about to leave, but He makes it clear that He'll be sending someone in His place.

Instead of having the Son of God down here teaching and directing them from the outside of their lives, they'll have the Spirit of God guiding and directing them from the *inside*. The very Spirit that Jesus has, the Spirit that empowers Him, will come and live inside them, allowing them to experience the same oneness, the same love, the same power with Jesus.

Not a bad deal. But, contrary to popular Eastern teachings, this oneness with God, this presence of His Spirit, comes only to those who have committed their lives to Jesus Christ. We are not born with Him inside us, *we have to receive Him first.*

Finally, Jesus promises that the disciples will have peace. But, not the peace the world gives. On the contrary, there will be storms and dark, painful times ahead for these guys. In fact, most scholars believe that every one of them was either imprisoned, executed, or exiled.

The peace Jesus gives will have very little to do with outward circumstances. Instead, it will come from the inside and will be so powerful that it won't make any difference what the world throws at them from the outside.

The peace Jesus offers is for us, too. Jesus never promised to take us around the storms of life. In fact, He promised just the opposite: "In this world you will have trouble" (John 16:33). But He does promise to take us through those storms in such a way that they can't touch us inside where we really live.

Regardless of the outward circumstances, way down in our hearts the storms of life will never destroy our peace. If we've given our lives to God, then down deep, where it really counts, it will always be smooth sailing.

Ultimate Action

✔ *Do you have time for God?* Or do you only have time for friends, romantic relationships, sports, phone calls, youth group activities...but relegate God to an "if I have time" status.

✔ *Have you felt a bit stressed lately?* If so, reevaluate your priorities. Worship God. Adore Him. When He moves back in as your first love, then His amazing peace will return to you.

ULTIMATE MISSION!

Week Ten

X

Believers
must
change
the
world!

Day 64: The Great Gardener

I am the vine, you are the branches. He who abides in Me, and I in him, bears much fruit; for without Me you can do nothing (John 15:5 NKJV).

Ultimate Word: *Read John 15:1-17*

Ultimate Encounter

God is the expert gardener. He knows exactly what we need to grow strong and healthy. Even when the best areas in our lives are being trimmed or cut back, we have to trust that He knows what He's doing. The pruning will always—always!—be for our own good. No matter how painful it is, God's pruning will always help us grow strong and have the greatest amount of fruit. Besides the pruning, there's another important part to our growth.

The quality and productivity of our lives directly depends on our relationship with Jesus. "I am the vine, you are the branches," Jesus tells us. If a branch is severed, it cannot bear fruit. It can strain and strive all it wants, but if it's not connected to the tree it will be fruitless and eventually die. On the other hand, if a branch is strongly connected to a tree, the flow of life will be steady, making the branch strong and productive. If it is securely connected, the branch will be as strong and fruitful as the tree itself.

The important question we need to ask is: How strong is our connection? What can improve our connection with Jesus?

Ultimate Action

✔ *Grow your faith.* Jesus encountered many religious phonies. He called them "whitewashed tombs, which look beautiful on the outside but on the inside are full of dead men's bones..." (Matthew 23:27). If you feel uncomfortable about an area of your life, God is trying to get your attention. He wants you to be securely connected to the life-giving vine. Spend time in prayer. Ask Him to transform you into a 100-percent-genuine, fruit-bearing Christian.

✔ *Trust the Master Gardener.* God loves His children, but He hates sin. Remember: "If we confess our sins, he is faithful and just and will forgive us our sins and purify us from all unrighteousness" (1 John 1:9). Once you confess your sins, be prepared to let Jesus go to work on your life, pruning away the dead branches and making room for new growth.

✔ *Be patient.* The more you seek Jesus, the more He'll live His life through you. Keep looking at Christ. With time, He'll teach you the truth of Galatians 2:20: "I have been crucified with Christ and I no longer live, but Christ lives in me."

Day 65: Enemy of the State

If the world hates you, keep in mind that it hated me first. If you belonged to the world, it would love you as its own. As it is, you do not belong to the world, but I have chosen you out of the world. That is why the world hates you (John 15:18,19).

Ultimate Word: *Read John 15:18-27*

Ultimate Encounter

Jesus says, "You are my friends if you do what I command." If we obey and stay in His love, we're no longer just His servants—we are His friends!

Picture it: The Creator of the universe, the one who is receiving all that glory and power from the Father, the very being that all of the angels and creation worship—*He has chosen to call you His friend.*

But there's a little thorn. If we're friends with God, the world will hate us. It's a sad fact, but it's the truth. The world hated Jesus enough to kill Him, so why should we, His followers, expect things to be any different?

There is one way we can avoid the persecution: Fake it. We can turn into secret-agent Christians going undercover. That way we can have the best of both worlds—a little of God here, a little of the world there. But being friends with the world means compromising our beliefs by going along with the crowd. This means denying Jesus—if not in word then at least in deed. And the Bible has a few serious words for those of us who try to play it both ways: "You adulterous people, don't you know that friendship with the world is hatred toward God? Anyone who chooses to be a friend of the world becomes an enemy of God" (James 4:4).

As Christians, we have two choices: 1) pursue God's love or 2) pursue the world's love. The decision isn't easy. But since it comes down to being loved by one or the other, we have to ask ourselves whose love we really want. Whose love is deeper and more committed?

Do we want to be loved by a world that basically wants to use us? A world that, as soon as we make a false step or fall from its grace, is going to wad us up and toss us away like a used tissue?

Or do we want to be loved by someone whose dedication is so intense, so committed that He considered our lives more important than His own?

When you look at it this way, the decision doesn't seem so difficult.

Ultimate Action

Even if you're a Christian, it can be hard to say no to the world. So what can you do? Decide what values God wants you to follow *before* you're in a tight spot. If you plan your responses ahead of time, and have your values grounded in God's Word, resisting the world is a lot easier.

Day 66: Tough Times

They will make you outcasts from the synagogue, but an hour is coming for everyone who kills you to think that he is offering service to God (John 16:2 NASB).

Ultimate Word: *Read John 16:1-4*

Ultimate Encounter

Jesus doesn't take any chances. So far, the disciples haven't demonstrated a real firm grasp of who He is or what His mission is all about. So, just to be sure, He goes over it one last time. He wants them to realize that the world is going to hate them. In fact, according to Jesus, the hatred will be so intense that people will think they're doing God a favor by killing them. (History proves this out. During those first few decades of Christianity alone, Christians were beaten, tortured, and killed.)

Today people are still persecuting Christians. In some places it's not as obvious as others, but it's there. They did it to God, so it shouldn't be too great a shock when they do it to us. More than 200 million Christians around the world today are experiencing severe persecution. For some, simple acts of worship or home Bible study has resulted in imprisonment and even death.

In the Sudan, for example, the government has engaged in a coordinated campaign of systematic murder, starvation, crucifixion, infanticide, and child enslavement, which is causing the deaths of more than one million Christians and other religious minorities. This shocking report comes from Christian Freedom International (CFI), an organization that monitors religious persecution throughout the world. CFI also reports that the government of China, in response to the growing and still illegal "house church" movement, has declared its official policy to be the "need to strangle th[is] baby while it is still in the manger."

It is crucial that the body of Christ *act now* on the call expressed in Hebrews 13:3: "Remember those in prison as if you were their fellow prisoners, and those who are mistreated as if you yourselves were suffering."

Ultimate Action

✔ *Pray.* Intercede for the men, women, and children being brutally persecuted.

✔ *Support a Christian ministry dedicated to reaching out.* Actively get involved in helping those in the world who are poor, hungry, and persecuted. (Compassion International and World Vision are two possibilities. Ask your pastor for other suggestions.)

✔ *Be prepared.* The next time someone makes a "harmless" little joke about your faith or when you're left behind for being a "Holy Joe" or "Holy Josephine," don't take it too hard. In fact, take it as a compliment! After all, it was done to Jesus— and that puts you in some pretty good company.

Day 67: Work of the Spirit

But when he, the Spirit of truth, comes, he will guide you into all truth. He will not speak on his own; he will speak only what he hears, and he will tell you what is yet to come (John 16:13).

Ultimate Word: *Read John 16:5-16*

Ultimate Encounter

In today's passage, Jesus reminds His followers that He's going away. He also repeats His promise to send the Holy Spirit to help those who believe. But then He goes on to explain that the Spirit also has another assignment: to help the rest of the world know God's truth.

How will the Holy Spirit convince people they need God? He'll do this in three ways:

1. *Conviction of Sin*

Until we know that we need forgiveness, we won't ask for forgiveness. And without that forgiveness we're sunk. So the Holy Spirit's first job is to convince the world how horrible sin is and how desperately people need Jesus.

2. Conviction of Christ's Righteousness

Most people think they've got it pretty well together: "Hey, I'm righteous. I don't kill or cheat or steal. I even buy Girl Scout cookies from time to time." But when compared with Jesus' righteousness (who's so perfect that He's sitting beside His Father in heaven), well, let's just say our goodness doesn't quite stack up.

So the Holy Spirit's second job is to convince the world that our definition of real good is not good enough. What God demands is perfection. And since Jesus is the only one who is perfect, we'd better make sure it's His righteousness the Father sees when we stand in front of God's throne on judgment day. We'd better make sure it's Jesus' goodness that God will judge us by—not our own.

3. Conviction of Truth

Everyone (including the devil) will be judged before God's throne. And since the Holy Spirit is continually doing His first two jobs—convicting people of their sins and showing them Christ's righteousness—many people have and will drop to their knees to cry out for help. It is that conviction that will lead many to seek Jesus Christ and ask for salvation before it's too late.

Ultimate Action

✔ *Don't sit still!* Consider how enormously expanded the kingdom of God would be if each Christian reached just one person. But too often believers get sedated and so comfortable that they do nothing for the Lord. Some people even argue, "It's not *our* job to save the world; Jesus already did that." But consider this: We are His hands and His feet. If we don't do it, it won't get done.

✔ *Reach out.* Think of someone in your life who doesn't have a relationship with Jesus (a family member, a friend at school, a teacher). Now do the following:

—Spend some time during this month praying for this person's salvation.

—Do your best to live your faith and walk your talk, especially when you're around this person.

—Look for opportunities to share Christ with this person: an Easter production at church, youth camp, a Super Bowl party. When the moment is right (the Holy Spirit will help you know when), don't hesitate. Go for it!

Day 68: Grief to Joy

These things I have spoken to you, that in Me you may have peace. In the world you will have tribulation; but be of good cheer, I have overcome the world (John 16:33 NKJV).

Ultimate Word: *Read John 16:17-33*

Ultimate Encounter

The disciples are *still* having a tough time figuring out exactly what's going on. So Jesus *again* explains that He's leaving for a little while (His death and later His ascension), but that He'll shortly return (His resurrection and ultimately His second coming). It's going to be tough while He's gone but He assures them that, like childbirth, the pain will definitely be worth the gain.

Jesus encourages His disciples to ask the Father for *anything* in His name. If they do, He'll see to it that they get it—no ifs, ands, or buts. If they ask for anything in Jesus' name, it's theirs. Not a bad deal—and one that still applies today.

But before you build an extra garage for all your Corvettes and Jaguars or start writing your Academy Awards® acceptance speech, keep in mind that our requests have to be *in His name.* That doesn't mean we come to God with our shopping lists, slap on an "in Jesus' name I pray" (as if it were some sort of celestial postage stamp), and mail our requests off to Him.

"In Jesus' name" means just that. We are asking for things that are representational of who Jesus is. We are asking for things that fit into His will and His desires for us here on earth. God is not a genie who has to answer our every whim and desire because we use "magic words."

But if our hearts are right and our motivations are right, then Jesus means exactly what He says: "I tell you the truth, my Father will give you whatever you ask in my name" (John 16:23).

Finally the disciples start to catch on. At last they think they understand what Jesus is talking about.

Well, not quite... .

When they finally figure they're up to speed and start pledging their undying allegiance to Him, Jesus has a little bad news.

"You're all going to desert Me."

And, regardless of what they say, they will.

You know, the nice thing about the disciples is that every time we get to thinking we're lousy Christians—bottom-of-the-heap losers—all we have to do is see who Jesus picked as His best friends here on earth. Suddenly we don't feel so bad; suddenly we realize He's used to our kind.

Ultimate Action

Find a quiet place away from the phone, the TV, the stereo, and any other distraction. Talk to Jesus friend to friend. Pour out your heart. Tell Him all your hopes and dreams and desires. And as you pray, remember: Give God the grains of your life, and He'll give you back His entire beach!

Day 69: Heart of Hearts

Now this is eternal life: that they may know you, the only true God, and Jesus Christ, whom you have sent (John 17:3).

Ultimate Word: *Read John 17:1-19*

Ultimate Encounter

Probably no other section of Scripture more accurately captures the heart and deepest desires of Jesus than today's passage. For the first time, Jesus lets the disciples (and us) eavesdrop on His most intimate conversation with His Father. Let's break His prayer down so we can better study it.

Jesus Prays for Himself

First He asks to be glorified "with the glory I had with you before the world began" (John 17:5). Jesus is not on a power trip here. He knows He is about to face more agony than any human being has ever faced in the history of the world—not just the pain of the cross, but also the suffering and punishment for all the world's sins. For those few hours He'll literally be carrying the weight of the entire world on His shoulders.

And Jesus knows one other thing. He knows He can back out and call it quits any time He wants. So He's also praying for the strength and courage to go through with it, to succeed in paying the price. If He does, there is no more perfect demonstration of God's love for us or of His Son's immense glory.

Jesus Prays for the Disciples

Next, Jesus prays for His friends. First He asks for unity. It's as if He already knows the centuries of arguments and fights that are going to plague the church—everything from wars over major doctrines to hurt feelings about what color the curtains in the church bathroom should be.

Next, because the world will hate them, He prays for His followers to have the "full measure" of His joy. Again Jesus makes it clear that real joy doesn't depend on outward circumstances. Real joy comes from the depth of our relationships with God.

Jesus Prays for Protection

Finally, Jesus asks the Father to protect the disciples from the world. He asks His Father not to take His followers out of the world, but to protect them while they're in it.

There's a fine balance shown in Jesus' prayer. God does not want us to huddle together like a bunch of scared sheep, afraid to associate with the world. But at the same time, He doesn't want us to get sucked into the world and be destroyed by it.

There are so many people out there. And Jesus wants to save them. They're not the enemy; they're only prisoners of the enemy. But how can we help them if we hide out? What good is salt if it stays in the saltshaker? What good is light if it never leaves the light bulb?

We all know Christians who are so busy running around with their Christian friends from Christian event to Christian event that they never reach out, they never impact the world. But there's the other type too—the Christian who is so busy chasing after the world that he or she eventually gets caught by it. The trick is to find the middle ground.

Ultimate Action

The goal is a balance. Yes, you are to associate with the world to make it better. But if you're just using that as an excuse for worldly thrills, then it may be time for a little reevaluation.

We must change the world—instead of letting it change us.

Day 70: Peace in the Pasture

I have given them the glory that you gave me, that they may be one as we are one: I in them and you in me. May they be brought to complete unity to let the world know that you sent me and have loved them even as you have loved me (John 17:22,23).

Ultimate Word: *Read John 17:20-26*

Ultimate Encounter

Jesus' prayer continues as He lifts up the ones who will come after the disciples—that's us and every Christian through the centuries. Again He asks that we will be one, just as He and the Father are one.

He doesn't ask that we all become assembly-line Christians. He doesn't want a bunch of Jesus clones, all thinking, acting, and dressing the same way. But He does ask for us to keep drawing closer and closer to the Father until we all wind up with the same kind of heart.

Keep in mind that there's nothing wrong with diversity among Christians. Diversity is good. Otherwise we'd all be the same person trying to do the same thing. Instead, as 1 Corinthians 12 explains, we're all *different parts* of the same body. One person may be the right hand; another may be the left little toe. All of us have different functions and different needs. Yet we all are vital to God's plan.

If we're committed to Christ, we all have one thing in common: We have the heart of God. And as we listen to that heart, as we become more and more in tune with what His Spirit teaches, we become more in tune with one another. It's not something we work up a sweat about; it just happens naturally. A.W. Tozer put it best in his classic book *The Pursuit of God* (Tyndale Publishing):

> Has it ever occurred to you that one hundred pianos all tuned to the same fork are automatically tuned to each other? They are of one accord by being tuned, not to each other, but to another standard to which each one must individually bow. So one hundred worshippers met together, each one looking away to Christ, are in heart nearer to each other than they could possibly be were they to become "unity" conscious and turn their eyes away from God to strive for closer fellowship.

Ultimate Action

✔ *Be a peacemaker among the body.* Strive to promote togetherness at home, at church, at youth group. How? For a clue, check out Ephesians 4:1-3: "As a prisoner for the Lord, then, I urge you to live a life worthy of the calling you have received. Be completely humble and gentle; be patient, bearing with one another in love. Make every effort to keep the unity of the Spirit through the bond of peace."

✔ *Handle quarrels and conflicts among believers.* How? Understand that *no* problem is too big for God to handle—not even a conflict with a buddy at church. God will set you on the right course if you let Him. Seek unity and solutions to problems, not strife and pointless quarrels.

ULTIMATE Payment!

Week Eleven

Journey
to the
cross
and see
how Jesus,
God's
sinless
sacrifice,
made it
possible
for us
to be
forgiven.

Day 71: The Arrest

Then Jesus answered and said to them, "Have you come out, as against a robber, with swords and clubs to take Me? I was daily with you in the temple teaching, and you did not seize Me. But the Scriptures must be fulfilled" (Mark 14:48,49 NKJV).

Ultimate Word: *Read Mark 14:43-52*

Ultimate Encounter

Jesus is done. He's briefed the disciples on all the basics. Now it's time to head for the Garden of Gethsemane to begin the final phase, to begin what He really came here to do in the first place. Jesus is about to go through the greatest torture and agony any human has ever undergone. He's about to suffer for *all* the sins of humanity. All of the penalty for our wrongdoings is about to be put on Him. The horror of what He's facing is so overpowering that He literally throws Himself to the ground, not once, but several times, begging the Father to find some other way.

Three times He pleads for the Father to call the whole thing off (Mark 14:32-36). He doesn't have to go through with this. He's innocent; He didn't foul up the world with sin, we did. So why should He suffer? And yet there's His deep, deep love for us.

It's a tremendous, agonizing battle. Three times the fate of the world hangs in the balance. Three times He nearly calls the whole thing off. The battle is so intense and ex-cruciating that, according to Luke 22:44, tiny capillaries began to explode near the surface of His skin, causing Him to sweat not only water but blood.

And the final outcome?

His love is so great that He'll go through whatever agony He needs to in order to save us. Picture it. God, caring more for our lives than for His own.

Judas and the soldiers arrive at the Garden. But just to make it clear that He is going under His own authority and not man's, Jesus announces His identity, and somehow the power of that statement literally knocks all of them to the ground (see John 18:5,6). The very men who are about to arrest and kill Jesus suddenly find themselves on their faces before Him.

Next, good old Peter tries to fight off all the soldiers with one sword (atta boy, Pete), but succeeds only in hacking off somebody's ear. Jesus orders him to stop, and Luke's Gospel tells us that He actually reaches out and heals the ear (22:50,51). He's come to do the Father's will: to save and heal—even those who are about to kill Him. Even though Jesus gave Himself up without struggle, yet He was totally in control of the situation.

The fact is, science and technology can't save us; not even all the money in the world can save us. Our only hope is Jesus and the price He paid on the cross—His life! Now it's up to us to believe...and accept His gift of eternal life.

Ultimate Action

Do you ever think of Jesus as weak during those final days? Don't! He is the powerful Son of God who is in control of the entire universe. Consider:

✔ He has power over His enemies.

✔ He has the power to lay down His life and the power to take it back again.

✔ He has the power to defeat Satan.

✔ He has the power to free us from sin.

✔ He has the power to create and to heal.

✔ He has the power to transform the lives of believers.

Now that's power!

Day 72: Truth on Trial

"He is worthy of death," they answered. Then they spit in his face and struck him with their fists. Others slapped him and said, "Prophesy to us, Christ. Who hit you?" (Matthew 26:66-68).

Ultimate Word: *Matthew 26:57–27:10*

Ultimate Encounter

At daybreak, Jesus is brought before the Sanhedrin (the top religious leaders of the country). They desperately look for evidence against Jesus so they can put Him to death, but they can't find any. Then two witnesses come forward.

"This fellow said, 'I am able to destroy the temple of God and rebuild it in three days.'"

The high priest stands up, looks at Jesus, and says, "Are you not going to answer? What is this testimony that these men are bringing against you?" But Jesus remains silent.

The priest gets impatient: "Tell us if you are the Christ, the Son of God."

Jesus finally answers, "Yes, it is as you say."

The priest tears his clothes and accuses Jesus of speaking blasphemy. The other officials say, "He is worthy of death." They spit in Jesus' face and strike Him with their fists.

One of the most amazing aspects of Jesus' trial is that it never occurred to any of them that His claim might be true. They had seen and witnessed His miracles and they marveled at His teachings. Yet these guys were so spiritually blind, they refused to see the truth. It is important that we acknowledge who Jesus is and give Him the glory and honor He deserves.

Ultimate Action

Imagine how alone Jesus must have felt. His friends doubted—and even betrayed—Him. And the very people He came to save spit in His face.

Do you ever feel as if the whole world has turned on you? You take a stand for God among nonbelievers, and your Christian pals split. In those moments, know that Christ is with you. In those times understand that victory for the believer is seldom in the shouting and showboating. It's usually in the quiet, day-to-day persistence of doing what you know is right—whether anyone sees it or not. Eventually the glory will come. It always does.

Day 73: Truth v. Popularity

And Pilate, wanting to release Jesus, addressed them again, but they kept on calling out, saying, "Crucify, crucify Him!" (Luke 23:20,21 NASB).

Ultimate Word: *Read Luke 23:13-31*

Ultimate Encounter

Since Israel is occupied by the Romans, the Jews have no say over who will live or die. So they have to take Jesus to the Roman in charge, Pontius Pilate.

Now, Pilate is a little nervous. His wife has just had a dream and warned him: "Don't have anything to do with that innocent man" (Matthew 27:19). Then, to make matters worse, when he tries to grill Jesus, the Lord turns the tables on him: "Is that your own idea...or did others talk to you about me?"

Jesus is even giving Pilate the opportunity to confess Him as Lord!

But, being the superb politician he is, Pilate sidesteps the question and repeats his own: "So You are a king?" (John 18:37 NASB). Christ answers clearly that He is, but not in the material sense that everyone is assuming. His is a different kingdom, the spiritual kingdom.

Pilate realizes that Jesus is no political threat, so he tells the leaders there is no basis for a charge against Him. There it is; that's the judgment. Pilate finds Jesus innocent. Yet because Pilate is more concerned about what people think than the truth, he refuses to stand up for what he believes.

But the Lord isn't done with him yet. He'll have other opportunities to get it right.

There are times in our lives when most of us have sold out. We've opted for popularity at the expense of truth. Maybe it's out-and-out denial of the truth like we've just seen with Peter. Or maybe it's going along with the crowd when we know it's wrong, as Pilate did. Whatever the case, most of us have done it.

Truth versus popularity. It's a tough decision sometimes. But, as we'll see with Peter and even with Pilate, it's a decision that Jesus will constantly help us with. It's a decision that He will give us chance after chance to get right.

Ultimate Action

✔ *Decide right now.* Live your life based on the fact that God's truth is more important to you than going along with what's popular.

✔ *Make a commitment.* Seek the truth instead of following current fads.

✔ *Ask God to help you.* He'll help you turn away from the whims of the world. Ask Him to give you the desire to get serious about living for Him.

Day 74: Payment Begins

Then Pilate took Jesus and had him flogged. The soldiers twisted together a crown of thorns and put it on his head. They clothed him in a purple robe and went up to him again and again, saying, "Hail, king of the Jews!" And they struck him in the face (John 19:1-3).

Ultimate Word: *Read John 19:1-16*

Ultimate Encounter

First, Jesus is flogged by a whip with multiple leather strips. Each strip has a sharp jagged piece of stone or metal tied at its end to make sure it digs nice and deep into the flesh.

Next, His captors weave a crown of thorns and jam it down on His head. And by thorns we're not talking your standard blackberry or rose variety. We're talking about a plant in that region whose thorns are about an inch long and as sharp as sewing needles.

They wrap a robe around Jesus' body, which by now looks like one big, open wound. Later, when the blood has dried to it, they'll rip it off. Remember the pain of removing a Band-Aid® sticking to a sore? Picture that over your whole body.

As a final insult, they begin spitting on Him and beating Him. In fact the soldiers get to playing a little game with Him, demanding that Jesus prophesy who will hit Him next as they punch Him in the face again and again and again.

Meanwhile, Pilate pleads with the religious officials, "I find no guilt in Him" (John 18:38 NASB).

Their response? "Crucify Him!"

Again Pilate turns to Jesus for help. But Jesus will not make Pilate's decision for him. The authority to make his decision about Christ is Pilate's and Pilate's alone.

God will not make our decisions about Jesus for us, either. It is up to us.

The screws tighten on Pilate as the religious leaders begin to call him a traitor to his country. "If you let this man go, you are no friend of Caesar!" (As if those religious leaders, who hate Rome, give a rip what Caesar thinks.) But this is not their only hypocrisy. In a final act of betrayal to God, these great religious leaders actually cry out, "We have no king but Caesar!" Caesar is their king. Not Christ, not God—Caesar!

And the sad fact of the matter is that they're right.

We need to evaluate how we are serving God. If He's not top priority—if He's not Lord—we need to make changes so we serve Him with all our hearts.

Ultimate Action

Don't be like the religious leaders of Christ's day. Jesus is your King. Spend time in prayer, telling Him how much you love Him and how much you need His guidance as you make decisions for your life.

Day 75: The Cost Escalates

And He, bearing His cross, went out to a place called the Place of a Skull, which is called in Hebrew, Golgotha, where they crucified Him, and two others with Him, one on either side, and Jesus in the center. Now Pilate wrote a title and put it on the cross. And the writing was: JESUS OF NAZARETH, THE KING OF THE JEWS (John 19:17-19 NKJV).

Ultimate Word: *Read John 19:17-27*

Ultimate Encounter

The cross was one of the most hideous forms of execution ever invented. And it was here, on a cross, that God made the final payment for our sins. Iron spikes are driven completely through each of Jesus' hands and feet. He is stripped naked and raised into the air for everyone to see and mock as He hangs for hours in the intense Middle Eastern sun.

Despite all of this, Jesus will not physically die from blood loss or heat prostration—that would be too easy. Instead, He will become so tired and filled with so much pain that no matter how hard He tries, He will not be able to hold His body up by His pierced feet. He will begin to hang from His torn hands, His weight gradually pulling His arms and shoulders from their sockets.

He'll try to keep shifting the strain back to His feet, but exhaustion will eventually overtake Him until, finally, He must hang completely by His arms. And it is at this time that His body will begin to slowly cave in on itself until He can't get enough air into His lungs.

And there, in the blistering heat, stripped of His clothing, body already swollen and bleeding from the floggings and beatings in the face, spikes driven through His hands and feet, bones popping out of His sockets, Jesus will, ever so slowly, physically die of suffocation.

In the history of our race, no one has outdone the Romans in inventing a more excruciating way to die. But what's amazing is that hundreds of years before the Romans even existed, King David prophesied in exact detail what it would be like for the Messiah: "A band of evil men has encircled me, they have pierced my hands and my feet. I can count all my bones; people stare and gloat over me. They divide my garments among them and cast lots for my clothing" (Psalm 22:16-18).

The Psalms passage is a pretty accurate description. Here's another, with a stronger emphasis on why: "He was pierced for our transgressions, he was crushed for our iniquities; the punishment that brought us peace was upon him, and by his wounds we are healed. We all, like sheep, have gone astray, each of us has turned to his own way; and the LORD has laid on Him the iniquity of us all" (Isaiah 53:5,6).

Ultimate Action

✔ *Are you feeling the pain of disappointment today?* Perhaps you were rejected by a friend or cut from the team. Christ understands; take your pain to Him.

✔ *Are you confused?* There are a lot of mixed messages the world blasts your way. Maybe a teacher is arguing that "creationism is make-believe," or a Christian friend is trying to convince you that smoking marijuana isn't a big deal to God. Christ will help you sort through the world's lies. He is the Author of truth. Ask Him for answers to your life problems.

✔ *Are you having trouble trusting?* Perhaps a parent walked out on you or a hero fell from grace. Christ will never let you down. Look at how much He paid for you on the cross. Take His hand, trust His promises, and lean on His shoulders for comfort. He'll hold you and carry you to a new level of trust.

Day 76: "It Is Finished"

When he had received the drink, Jesus said, "It is finished." With that, he bowed his head and gave up his spirit (John 19:30).

Ultimate Word: *Read John 19:28-37*

Ultimate Encounter

The death of Christ on the cross is one of history's most important moments. Since it's the key to whether people live or die, it's only natural that God referred to it throughout the Old Testament.

- ✔ Psalm 69:21 says He would be given gall in His food and vinegar to drink.

- ✔ Isaiah 53:12 says He would be killed among thieves.

- ✔ Psalm 34:20 says none of His bones would be broken.

- ✔ Isaiah 53:9 says He'd be buried in a rich man's tomb.

Keep in mind that all of these things were written *hundreds of years before Jesus ever made the scene.*

But the people around the cross saw even more than the fulfillment of prophecy during those hours. Nature itself began to cry out and writhe at what was happening to its

Creator. Sound weird? Matthew 27:45 explains that at the height of the execution, the sun was actually darkened from noon to 3 P.M. (No eclipse has ever lasted three hours.)

There was also a violent earthquake. Now we're not talking California-tremor time. This quake was so intense that it literally split rocks apart and opened up graves. And what happened to the bodies that were buried in those graves? "The tombs broke open and the bodies of many holy people who had died were raised to life. They came out of the tombs, and after Jesus' resurrection they went into the holy city and appeared to many people" (Matthew 27:52,53).

As a grand finale, the veil in the temple ripped in two (Luke 23:45). That may not sound like much of a finale to you, but to the Jewish people of the day it was serious business. For one thing, the curtain was so thick (several inches) that it's doubtful any person or normal earthquake could have ripped it. Second, the curtain served as a barrier to protect the people from getting too close to God. You see, back then part of God's presence actually stayed in a room called the "holy of holies," which was separated from the rest of the temple by this thick curtain. God's holiness was so intense that if any of the common people went inside that room, they'd die on the spot. Only the high priest was allowed to enter and then only once a year. He had a rope tied around his ankles so he could be pulled out if he keeled over. In short, the curtain was a form of protection *and* separation.

But by Jesus' death, all that changed. Suddenly, the barrier is destroyed, ripped from top to bottom. Jesus' payment on the cross now makes it possible for anybody who accepts His offer of salvation to be pure enough to stand in God's presence.

God paid for the world's sins. The sacrifice, the substitution for our punishment for our disobedience, is complete. Jesus finishes all that He came to do. The mission is accomplished. We're free. The tremendous debt that each of us has run up in heaven has been paid in full by another.

Ultimate Action

Savor what you discovered in today's lesson: The debt has been paid. *Your sins have been forgiven!* It's time for joy! It's time for celebration! Spend some time in prayer and worship, thanking God for the gift of salvation: "Lord, I praise You for defeating sin and giving me eternal life. Help me claim that victory every day."

Day 77: The Burial

So Joseph [of Arimathea] brought some linen cloth, took down the body, wrapped it in the linen, and placed it in a tomb cut out of rock. Then he rolled a stone against the entrance of the tomb (Mark 15:46).

Ultimate Word: *Read Mark 15:42-47*

Ultimate Encounter

Two members of the Sanhedrin, Joseph of Arimathea and Nicodemus (secret followers of Jesus), are willing to risk persecution from their friends and ask Pilate for permission to bury the body. (See John 19:38-40 for more details.) They use Joseph's tomb, the one he had been planning to use for himself. As a result, we see another ancient prophecy being fulfilled. Isaiah 53:9 says: "He was assigned a grave with the wicked, and with the rich in his death."

There is very little time left before sundown (that's when the Sabbath begins), so they wrap the body in spices and linen and lay it in the tomb.

Like Joseph and Nicodemus, Jesus wants us to be gutsy about our faith. He wants us to be people of action, not just words. And consider this: Nowhere do we read of Peter's presence or of those who were so boastful about their allegiance to Jesus. Instead, the ones who are barely mentioned by name do what God asks without hoping to be in the spotlight.

Ultimate Action

Faith, obedience, even taking risks for His sake. This is what Jesus wants from you. Not just good intentions and smooth, Christian talk. He wants action. But stepping out in obedience not only involves risk to your reputation and the possibility of losing friends, it also doesn't guarantee that you're going to be in the spotlight. You might not get a pat on the back, but you will please God—and that's what matters most.

✔ Are you willing to take risks for God?

✔ Is pleasing Him your most important desire?

ULTIMATE Triumph!

Week Twelve

X

Be an
eyewitness
as Jesus
defeats
death
and
offers
the gift
of eternal
life
to all
who
follow Him.

Day 78: Death Dies

Now on the first day of the week Mary Magdalene went to the tomb early, while it was still dark, and saw that the stone had been taken away from the tomb. Then she ran and came to Simon Peter, and to the other disciple, whom Jesus loved, and said to them, "They have taken away the Lord out of the tomb, and we do not know where they have laid Him" (John 20:1,2 NKJV).

Ultimate Word: *Read John 20:1-10*

Ultimate Encounter

Jesus had been laid in the tomb, and women were going there to anoint Jesus' body with more spices. When they got there, the guards were laying like dead men and the stone was rolled away (see Matthew 28:1-11; Luke 24:10). When some of the guards got up, they raced to the chief priests with a crazy story about an earthquake at the tomb and an angel who rolled away the heavy stone. What do the priests do? They bribe the soldiers to lie! "Tell everyone that you fell asleep and that those pesky disciples stole the body. Above all, don't even mention the earthquake and the angel!"

If Jesus Christ did not rise from the dead, then everything He said and did would be a lie. Anybody can claim to be God—psychiatric hospitals are filled with such misguided people. But to say you're God and then *prove* you're immortal—that's another matter.

The resurrection was the proof, the seal of authenticity. Without it, Jesus would just be another egomaniac. For centuries people have tried to disprove the resurrection. And for centuries people have not only failed but during their research some have actually become Christians!

"Yeah," other people say, "but maybe Jesus wasn't really dead and just rolled away the stone Himself. Right, some guy that's been beaten, tortured, and mutilated for hours is going to lie unattended for two cold nights in a tomb and suddenly find the strength to roll away a two-ton rock, fight off all the Roman soldiers guarding it, and show up convincing everyone that He has a glorious resurrected body. I don't think so.

And while we're talking about His body, let's not forget the blood and water that flowed from His side when the soldier speared it on the cross. If He were alive, the wound would have spurted red blood. But in a dead body, the blood separates into massive red clots and watery serum, just as John described it (see John 19:34).

"Maybe the disciples moved it" some people say.

Okay, let's think this one through: A group of men who have dedicated their lives to a teacher who insisted on truth and honesty are suddenly going to turn into liars and swindlers. And each of these self-seeking no-goods will be willing to face poverty, incredible hardship, torture, and even death to perpetuate that lie. Not a chance.

Then there are the soldiers. Considering that Roman soldiers were the best fighting men in the world, it's not likely the disciples could overpower them and knock them out. But even if they could, why didn't they hurry and race off with the body before the soldiers came to, instead of painstakingly unwrapping all of the burial clothes and neatly folding the facecloth before making their getaway?

"O.K., so the soldiers did it."

Right, the very people who have been assigned to make sure Jesus' body isn't moved decide to make it happen. What a neat practical joke to pull on their superiors. Of course, it would mean their execution for becoming traitors, but what's a little death for a laugh or two?

While we're looking at evidence, let's not forget that Jesus' resurrection was something He had predicted time and time again. Then, of course, there were all those Old Testament prophecies.

Once we've looked at all the facts and carefully examined the arguments, we would need more faith to believe that Jesus did *not* rise from the grave than to believe that He did.

Ultimate Action

The death of death. That's exactly what happened on the cross. Your sinful nature was crucified on the cross with Jesus. That's right, the "old you" died, then Jesus raised to life the "new you." You are no longer under the power of sin. Jesus' death paid the price; His resurrection sets you free.

Does this mean you'll never sin again? Nope. But you are no longer under bondage to sin—if you choose not to let sin have control. You are now under

Christ's freeing power. Through Him, you have the strength to resist temptation and turn away from sin.

✔ Ask Jesus to help you break Satan's strongholds in your life.

✔ Tell Jesus that you want to be controlled by His spirit, not by sin.

✔ Confess your sin to Jesus the moment you mess up.

Day 79: Surprise Visits

A week later his disciples were in the house again, and Thomas was with them. Though the doors were locked, Jesus came and stood among them and said, "Peace be with you!" Then he said to Thomas, "Put your finger here; see my hands. Reach out your hand and put it into my side. Stop doubting and believe" (John 20:26, 27).

Ultimate Word: *Read John 20:10-31*

Ultimate Encounter

When the women ran back to tell the disciples the good news that Jesus was alive, they must have encountered a lot of doubt. "You've seen the Lord? Look, I hate to be the one to deliver bad news, but I think you women have been under way too much stress, and I think your imaginations are running wild."

"No, it's true! We saw Him with our own eyes!"

"Wake up already! Face the facts: He's dead. He was crucified and put in the grave."

"But the grave is empty. He's alive! Come see for yourself," was the women's reply.

For more than 40 days after His resurrection, Jesus visited His disciples and friends. In fact, according to 1 Corinthians 15:6, He appeared to more than 500 people at one time. But it was Jesus' closest friends who needed the most comfort. Their hopes and dreams had been shattered. Everything they had lived for and believed in for the last three years had literally died—or so they thought.

Jesus Appeared to Mary Magdalene

The first people Jesus appeared to were women. At the time women were often considered inferior, only good for making babies (especially if they were boy babies). And one of the women, Mary Magdalene, had a questionable past. (She had seven demons cast out [Mark 16:9].) This did not make her the world's most reputable person. (Once again we see Jesus going first to the low and humble.)

Jesus and the Disciples

Picture it: the disciples huddled together in fear behind locked doors. Their leader had been killed, and they are expecting the soldiers to come barging in to arrest them. Everything has fallen apart. They couldn't even give their Lord a decent burial because somebody stole the body. And to top it off, one of the women in their group has had some sort of nervous breakdown; going around telling everyone she has seen Jesus.

Thomas

Later, when Jesus appears to the others, Tom isn't around. And even though all of the disciples tell him the good news, Thomas refuses to believe: "Unless I see the nail marks in his hands and put my finger where the nails were, and put my hand into his side, I will not believe it" (John 20:25).

If that is what Thomas needs, that is what Thomas will get—to the letter. One week later, Jesus again appears behind locked doors and tells him to touch His wounds. "Stop doubting and believe," Jesus says. (See John 20:27.)

Thomas finally believes, and Jesus is glad enough, but He also points out that the ones who are really going to be blessed are the ones who haven't seen Him, yet still believe.

Ultimate Action

If ever there was a time of total hopelessness for the disciples, this was it. Which probably explains why Jesus chose this moment to make His appearance. And His first words? Probably what they needed more then anything else at the moment: "Peace be with you!"

✔ Understand that the Lord will give you peace during what feels like your toughest moments.

✔ Seek Jesus in times of stress. Don't operate on your own strength. Reach out to the Master.

Anyone can see and believe like Thomas. But to believe without seeing (like you)—that's major faith. As a result of this, you'll receive major blessings.

✔ Ask Jesus to wipe away your doubts.

✔ Take Him at His Word. Let go and trust Him.

Day 80: Miraculous Catch

Early in the morning, Jesus stood on the shore, but the disciples did not realize that it was Jesus. He called out to them, "Friends, haven't you any fish?"

"No," they answered.

He said, "Throw your net on the right side of the boat and you will find some." When they did, they were unable to haul the net in because of the large number of fish (John 21:4-6).

Ultimate Word: *Read John 21:1-14*

Ultimate Encounter

Today's passage is one of the most touching sections of Scripture. Not only does it show the humanness of Peter and the disciples, but it also captures Jesus' tenderness.

Peter and the guys are hanging out at the Sea of Tiberias (the one they used to fish from and walk on). Peter, who is still feeling pretty guilty about denying Jesus all those times, probably thinks he's good for nothing else but what he used to do, so he goes fishing. But he can't even do that right. All night they work and what do they catch? Zip.

Then, early in the morning, one of them spots this guy way off on the beach, starting a fire.

"Catch anything?" the guy shouts.

"Are you kidding?"

"Try throwing your net on the other side. I bet you'll find something there."

Now these guys are bone weary and no doubt pretty cranky. The last thing they need is for some landlubber to tell them how to fish. But there must have been something strangely familiar about this guy's voice because they give it a shot and wind up with more fish than they can haul in.

John (who never refers to himself by name in his Gospel) is the first to recognize who the stranger is. And as soon as he lets Peter know, old Pete cannonballs into the water (clothes and all) leaving the rest of the guys to fight with the fish. Sure, he cares about this incredible catch—after all, he is a fisherman. But that's his buddy, his Lord, on the shore there, and everything else pales by comparison.

Can't you see Jesus chuckling as this lumbering ox splashes through the water toward Him, oblivious of his friends' shouts and complaints about being left with all the work?

Later, they all sit around the fire and have a hot breakfast and no doubt a few laughs. A catch of 153 large fish is something worth celebrating. But you know, there is probably still a little uneasiness on Peter's part. The memory of denying Jesus all those times is still eating at him. There is a good chance he couldn't quite look Jesus in the eye.

But that is about to change.

Ultimate Action

Are you having trouble looking Jesus in the eye because of something you've done? Are your quiet times dry? Does Jesus seem distant? Do business with the Lord right now. *Don't delay.* Tell Him what's bugging you, and share your doubts, fears, frustrations, and failures. Ask Jesus to do the miraculous in your life. He will do it!

Day 81: Reconciliation

He said to him the third time, "Simon, son of John, do you love Me?" Peter was grieved because He said to him the third time, "Do you love Me?" And he said to Him, "Lord, You know all things; You know that I love You." Jesus said to him, "Tend My sheep" (John 21:17 NASB).

Ultimate Word: *Read John 21:15-25*

Ultimate Encounter

Now it's just Jesus and Peter one-on-one. "Simon," Jesus says, "Do you truly love me more than these?"

Ouch. Peter's mind is no doubt flashing back to his boastful claim in the Upper Room at the "last supper": "Hey, all these flakes may deny You, but not me, no way, uh-uh." That was followed just a few hours later by, "Are you crazy? I don't know the guy!"

To top it off, in this intimate encounter between the two of them, Jesus is not only questioning Peter's devotion but He's using the old name Peter had before Jesus changed it. It's as if He's forcing Peter to start from scratch. And Jesus doesn't ask just once. He asks three times. By the third time Peter's heart is breaking. "Lord, you know all things; you know that I love you." And for the third time, Jesus commands Peter to take care of His sheep.

Three times Peter denied Jesus in the courtyard. And three times Jesus has him confess his loyalty. It is a painful experience, but it is necessary to prove to the disciples *and to Peter* that he is back in the group, that Peter once again is assigned the task of looking out for others. It will not always be an easy job, but as long as Peter stays humble and depends on God's power instead of his own ego, he will succeed.

John ends his Gospel by explaining that Jesus did plenty of other things, but that he just doesn't have the space to write them all down. "If every one of them were written down, I suppose that even the whole world would not have room for the books that would be written" (John 21:25).

And Jesus' work continues today.

Ultimate Action

As you keep giving yourself over to God, as you keep letting Him have His way in your life, Jesus will keep on working *in* you and *through* you.

✔ Let Him continue to work *in* you, making you "mature and complete, not lacking anything" (James 1:4).

✔ Let Him continue to work *through* you, giving you the power and wisdom to share His life with others so they, too, can come to Him and be all that He created them to be.

Day 82: Road to Emmaus

And they said to one another, "Did not our heart burn within us while He talked with us on the road, and while He opened the Scriptures to us?" So they rose up that very hour and returned to Jerusalem, and found the eleven and those who were with them gathered together, saying, "The Lord is risen indeed, and has appeared to Simon!" (Luke 24:32-34 NKJV).

Ultimate Word: *Read Luke 24:13-35*

Ultimate Encounter

On the same day Jesus arose from the tomb, a couple of disciples are heading toward another city. They're talking about all that has taken place when Jesus joins them, disguised in some way.

He begins asking questions, testing them to find out how much they really understand about what has happened. The disciples stop and call the disguised Christ a real idiot: "Are you the only one unaware of these things?" they ask.

But Jesus plays along, asking the disciples to explain what has happened from their point of view. They begin to describe Jesus only as a prophet. This must pain the Lord a little after all He has said and done, but He lets them continue.

The disciples explain that they were hoping Jesus would free Israel, but three days ago He was killed. Now all of their dreams are smashed. And to make matters worse, some of the most respected women of their group are beginning to hallucinate, making up stories of how angels have supposedly talked to them, saying Jesus is alive.

Jesus finally sets them straight, pointing out how necessary it was that He suffer first. He then goes through all of the Old Testament prophecies that teach that the Messiah has to come and suffer for our sins. (This must have been quite a lengthy Bible study, going through those hundreds of prophecies!)

Imagine having the Author of the Bible teaching it to you! It must have been terrific to see Jesus, to listen to Him teach, to walk by His side, to talk with Him, and to ask Him questions. How much clearer everything would be, right? Not quite.

Back then, Jesus could only physically be at one place at one time. People had to go to that one place to reach Him. It's not like that today. We (who have asked Him to become our Lord) have the Holy Spirit inside of us, teaching and instructing us continually. Isn't it great that we have God as our own personal tutor? Jesus is no longer a person we have to meet in the flesh to understand.

Ultimate Action

It's one thing to walk beside Jesus on the road, but it's quite another to have His Spirit living inside you. Take advantage of His presence. When the Bible begins to seem boring or if there's something you don't understand, take the time to ask the Holy Spirit to make it interesting, to make it clear, to reveal more truth.

Day 83: "You Are Witnesses!"

He told them, "This is what is written: The Christ will suffer and rise from the dead on the third day, and repentance and forgiveness of sins will be preached in his name to all nations, beginning at Jerusalem. You are witnesses of these things. I am going to send you what my Father has promised; but stay in the city until you have been clothed with power from on high" (Luke 24:46-49).

Ultimate Word: *Read Luke 24:36-49*

Ultimate Encounter

The two disciples Jesus talked to on the road to Jerusalem raced to tell the rest of His followers. And just as they're getting into all they experienced, Jesus shows up.

Everyone becomes frightened, thinking He's a ghost. Jesus understands their fears and, to prove to them that He's not a ghost—that He's been physically resurrected from the dead—He tells them to touch Him. Still, the news seems too good to be true, and they're afraid to believe. Jesus again understands, and in His patience asks for some food to eat so they will know He has a physical body.

Then He opens their minds so they can understand the Scriptures. He begins another study, explaining how the Old Testament prophecies were fulfilled by His suffering for us.

He goes on to explain that repentance for forgiveness of sins must be proclaimed to the whole world, starting right there in Jerusalem.

The Spirit had empowered Jesus to do amazing miracles; it was even by the Spirit's power that the Father had raised Jesus from death. And now the Holy Spirit is empowering these followers to be ambassadors of the King, Jesus Christ.

Ultimate Action

Do you fully grasp how much Christ has forgiven you? Read Hebrews 8:7-13 and Psalm 103:12. Then—

✔ ask Jesus to help you comprehend His forgiveness for you.

✔ ask Him to help you forgive others.

✔ ask the Lord to show you how to tell others about His forgiveness.

Day 84: The Great Commission

All authority in heaven and on earth has been given to me. Therefore go and make disciples of all nations, baptizing them in the name of the Father and of the Son and of the Holy Spirit, and teaching them to obey everything I have commanded you. And surely I am with you always, to the very end of the age (Matthew 28:18-20).

Ultimate Word: *Read Matthew 28:16-20*

Ultimate Encounter

After worshiping Jesus on the mountain near Galilee, and despite the fact that some disciples still have doubts in their hearts, Jesus commissions His followers. He tells them to go into the world and "make disciples of all nations... teaching them to obey everything I have commanded you."

Then the time has come for Him to leave, to prepare a place for us in heaven and to send the Holy Spirit to us. He rises up into the clouds with the promise that He'll return in exactly the same way (see Luke 24:50-53; Matthew 24:30,31; John 14:2).

We may feel pretty inadequate at times, but Jesus has commissioned us, too. He wants us to go and tell. There's a dying world out there that needs hope; the hope we have through Jesus Christ.

It's hard to swallow, but those who don't know Christ are *spiritually dead and are on their way to hell.* Is that a motivator or what! And remember, Satan is very motivated to keep us from being concerned about the lost. Even though the war has been won by Jesus, the devil is determined to destroy as many lives as he can until Christ returns.

The enemy hates it when we become burdened for the world. He knows that we'll begin to pray, give, and even go to the ends of the earth to share the good news about Jesus Christ. So Satan will do anything he can to divert our attention.

But keep in mind that *Christ is greater than the enemy.* And with the Lord's help, so are we! Christ has put the Holy Spirit inside each of us, and every minute of every day, if we let Him, He'll continue to teach, guide, protect, and above all, love us.

Ultimate Action

Spend time in prayer. Ask Jesus to protect you and help you beat the schemes of the devil. Ask Him to give you a heart and passion for evangelism: "Lord God, open my ears and eyes to the lost. Show me who to reach and give me the words that will open their eyes. Amen."